40

BLOWING SMOKE

BLOWING SMOKE

Rethinking the War on Drugs without Prohibition and Rehab

Michael J. Reznicek

ROWMAN & LITTLEFIELD PUBLISHERS, INC.
Lanham • Boulder • New York • Toronto • Plymouth, UK

Published by Rowman & Littlefield Publishers, Inc.
A wholly owned subsidiary of The Rowman & Littlefield Publishing Group, Inc.
4501 Forbes Boulevard, Suite 200, Lanham, Maryland 20706
http://www.rowmanlittlefield.com

Estover Road, Plymouth PL6 7PY, United Kingdom

British Library Cataloguing in Publication Information Available

Library of Congress Cataloging-in-Publication Data

Reznicek, Michael J., 1958-
  Blowing smoke : rethinking the war on drugs without prohibition and rehab
/ Michael J. Reznicek.
      p. cm.
  Includes bibliographical references and index.
  ISBN 978-1-4422-1514-6 (cloth : alk. paper) — ISBN 978-1-4422-1516-0
(electronic)
  1. Drug abuse—United States—Prevention—History. 2. Drug control—United
States—History. 3. Drug traffic—United States—History. I. Title.
  HV5825.R484 2011
  362.29'160973—dc23   2011043766

∞™ The paper used in this publication meets the minimum requirements of
American National Standard for Information Sciences—Permanence of Paper
for Printed Library Materials, ANSI/NISO Z39.48-1992.

Printed in the United States of America

To families who have been affected by substance abuse and are looking for answers.

CONTENTS

CONTENTS

ACKNOWLEDGMENTS

I am indebted to my wife, Linda, who has contributed to the philosophical development of this book. I am also grateful to the many friends and family members with whom I have been privileged to debate human nature—both its beauty and its sordidness.

INTRODUCTION

There is a growing realization that the drug war has failed. It has led to rampant violence and overcrowded prisons while failing to curtail drug use. Parts of Mexico have become extremely dangerous as drug cartels compete to fill the U.S. demand for narcotics.

Because of the harm caused by prohibition, many are calling for a new approach, and a consensus is building that we need to decrease the demand for drugs. Politicians, law enforcement officials, and medical experts say that we need to send more addicts through drug rehabilitation.

As enlightened as this plan sounds, more rehab is not the solution. More rehab could make matters worse. There is a solution to the drug problem, but it goes unnoticed. We are blinded by our devotion to the disease model of substance abuse.

The disease model arose from the progressive political tradition of the early twentieth century, when politicians wanted scientific solutions for social problems. Drug and alcohol abuse, which until that time had been viewed as a character problem, was redefined as a brain disease. This revolutionary change produced the drug rehab industry and the common belief that this was a job for professionals.

The problem is that the new approach never arose from scientific research. It was developed by a group of individuals who were sensitive to the prevailing political winds. They were the early members of Alcoholics Anonymous, and they promoted the disease theory to boost their membership rolls. The scientific community eventually got on board but only after federal and state governments forced the issue. The science was shaped to get the funding.

At first glance, the science can look compelling. Everyone has seen the colorful images of brain scans showing the effects of drugs on the brain. The images typically depict the biological correlates of craving and withdrawal symptoms, which increase the urge to use drugs. Disease experts claim that these urges cause a loss of control and force users into states of compulsive use.

Here is where an overreliance on scientific models misses the bigger picture. Whether people satisfy their urges depends in large part on what they perceive to be the consequences of their actions. This is as true for the heroin addict as it is for the toddler—there exist consequences that, when compelling enough, will redirect the behavior of each. This accounts for the widespread observation that substance abusers do not change until they "hit bottom," the point where the consequences of drug use finally outweigh its benefits. When people quit, their brains gradually return to their normal states, and craving and withdrawal symptoms fade away.

The disease model fails to account for the tremendous resourcefulness of human nature, and it leads to important unintended consequences. While rehab experts claim to be treating the urges, they are only changing the consequences—and in ways that *enable* the drug habit. Addicts learn that substance abuse is a brain disease and that relapses are part of the illness. They are told that they have genetic defects. They begin to see themselves as victims. They gain access to tangible benefits, such as welfare, health care, disability payments, food stamps, and other subsidies. The disease model also provides an excuse for all the wild, destructive things done under the influence—everything is now a symptom of the disease. The take-home message for addicts: "You're not responsible for your behavior." We enable addictions and then wonder why there are so many addicts.

I have practiced psychiatry for over twenty years and have attempted to help hundreds of substance abusers. I have experienced substance abuse in close family members and was once a substance abuser myself. No aspect of this problem is foreign to me.

The solution to the drug problem is to turn back the clock. Alcohol, opiates, cocaine, and marijuana have been used and abused for millennia. Prior to the disease model, societies had a workable solution: let people consume what they want and let informal cultural controls reinforce responsible behavior. Legal sanctions were reserved for any use that affected the safety of others. This approach was not trendy, and it was not scientific, but it forced people to moderate their use. With no enabling and no excuses, there was much less drama about drugs than there is today.

Adopting my proposal will require a tectonic shift in the way most people think. To that end, I will spend the better part of the book debunking the disease model. This is necessary because the medical profession has established itself in most people's minds as being the authority on human behavior. The profession has built citadels of research that appear to show that the disease model is the correct approach. This body of knowledge, though, is largely inaccessible to laypeople. If readers are to reject it, they will need to be acquainted with what the research actually shows. Simply offering another approach will seem reckless if people think that it is violating well-established science.

Some will recoil from my proposal because there is something intuitively pleasing in seeking "help" for loved ones, which is always more palatable than holding them responsible for their behavior. But when people begin to see the disease model's house-of-cards, they will learn that real help is much closer to home.

Others will argue that I am stigmatizing substance abusers. This will produce images of drunkards tied to colonial-era stocks. The American Psychiatric Association, for instance, claims that to look at substance abuse as anything but a disease is to stigmatize addicts.[1]

The problem with this objection is that it creates a false dichotomy: one is either compassionate and supports the disease model, or one is mean-spirited and rejects it. Competing models are conveniently squeezed out of the conversation. While I do advocate punishment for children who use drugs, I propose a set of cultural controls for adults that honors the freedom to self-indulge while respecting the rights of others not to subsidize or enable it. Charges of stigmatization, though, are politically useful; they effectively shield the profession from criticism and have done so for many years.

I have divided the book into three sections. Chapters 1 through 4 explore the history of the disease model and prohibition laws. There was a nineteenth-century physician-led disease model that never gained momentum because it took a backseat to the more popular temperance movement. And like many biological theories of the time, it gravitated toward eugenics. The modern disease model, on the other hand, was a lay movement that had to work hard to gain the support of the medical profession.

Drug prohibition laws originally were based on racist and anti-immigrant sentiments, but they were later co-opted to support the disease model: if drug abuse is a disease, then drugs are pathogens that need to be banned.

Chapters 5 through 8 review the science used to support the disease model. This is built on claims of abnormal dysfunction in two major areas: genetics and neurochemistry. Each will be addressed in detail, and I will argue that the neuroscientific knowledge that we have does not prove that substance abuse is a disease; it only shows why quitting can be hard.

The most compelling critique of the disease model will be found in the chapters that deal with drug rehab and rehab outcomes. I argue that medical treatment of substance abuse is not treatment at all but is more akin to ideological indoctrination into the disease model. Outcome studies are designed to show success even if none exists. I make the case that treatment can actually make the problem worse. Call substance abuse a disease if you must but don't treat it like one.

The final section presents a new way to look at drug abuse—the habit model. Unlike diseases, habits are built on normal psychological and physiological processes. Habits are practiced as long as they bring comfort and are abandoned when they cause pain. And all habits make changes to the brain. Whether one spends time smoking cocaine or practicing a musical instrument, the brain undergoes predictable changes based on the demands placed on it. This is known as neuroplasticity. Stop practicing a habit, and those changes go away. Toward the end of the book, I propose a way to help addicts develop whatever neuroplasticity they need to practice moderation.

Under the habit model, drug counselors would still have a role to play, but their focus would be radically changed. Instead of teaching the disease model and probing psychological dynamics, counselors would teach addicts about the nature of habits, neuroplasticity, and the incredible resourcefulness of human nature. Counselors would also serve as consultants to families and employers to help them find creative ways to incentivize responsible drug use.

Chapter 13 addresses common fears about drug legalization but also shows how the habit model presents new opportunities for understanding and responding to other deviant behaviors.

Throughout the book, alcohol, tobacco, and street drugs will be treated alike. Neurochemically, they have similar effects; they all stimulate the brain's reward pathways. The fact that alcohol is legal but cocaine is not has nothing to do with science and everything to do with politics.

1

MURDER, THIEVERY, AND DRUNKENNESS

The disease model of substance abuse dates to the early 1800s, when the spirit of the Enlightenment was very much alive. Reason and naturalistic explanations were replacing faith and revelation.

Human behavior and what motivated it were hotly debated. Explanations based on good and evil spirits were in decline, giving center stage to those holding rationalistic or naturalistic positions. Do humans behave as rational beings, or do they just follow the dictates of their own biology?

Colonial Americans held a mainly rational view of behavior, even if it was framed in a religious narrative. Drunkenness was considered a choice that people made. Thus, Puritan ministers spoke of the "sin" of drunkenness, as in Increase Mather's 1673 sermon "Wo to Drunkards." Alcohol per se was not evil, only its misuse. Reverend Mather wrote, "Drink is in itself a good creature of God, and to be received with thankfulness."

Historian Harry G. Levine has noted that whether colonials viewed habitual drunkenness as acceptable behavior or as a sin, drunkards were never considered to have "lost control" of their behavior, a central tenet of the disease model that was soon to come.[1] But Levine notes that as early as the mid-1700s, some must have been raising the loss-of-control issue because the famous evangelist Jonathan Edwards felt compelled to address it in his 1754 treatise *Freedom of the Will*. Edwards argued that words such as "irresistible" or "unable" could not be used in reference to moral choices.

From the colonial period to the 1830s, America's cities swelled with immigrants and rural transfers. Not surprisingly, there was a rise in pauperism, prostitution, street brawls, and workplace absenteeism. There were growing fears that the young country and its new industrial economy simply could not tolerate such problems, all of which seemed to be associated with heavy drinking.

In this setting, two movements arose to combat drunkenness. One was the temperance movement, which was the Protestant Church's response to the problem. The other came from the medical profession, which advocated a new disorder called "diseases of the will." While the two movements might appear unrelated, they were mutually reinforcing in early nineteenth-century America. Interestingly, this mix of religion and science is still a big part of our current approach to substance abuse.[2]

DISEASES OF THE WILL

The early disease model can be traced to Benjamin Rush (1745–1813), a Philadelphia physician and signer of the Declaration of Independence. In his *Inquiry into the Effects of Ardent Spirits upon the Human Body and Mind*,[3] he articulated the first organized view of drunkenness as a disease. Rush limited the disease to the abuse of spirits. He actually recommended the consumption of wine, beer, and fermented cider.

Rush was a leading advocate of the then-emerging concept of "diseases of the will." At the time, doctors stepped beyond treating physical problems and claimed to be able to treat human behavior. The concept was rather straightforward. Since human behavior was driven by the human will and the will was an emanation of the brain, it was only natural to conclude, for those drawn to naturalistic explanations, that the "will" must be diseased in cases of aberrant or criminal behavior.

The theory of a diseased will was warmly greeted in many circles, as it fit the enlightened philosophy of the age. It departed from faith and mysticism, but it also departed from rationalism. The fact that it sounded so scientific accorded it instant respect.

During the nineteenth century, no part of the brain could be identified as the "will," and in almost all cases of abnormal behavior, no brain pathology was ever found. Yet this did not dampen enthusiasm for the concept. If the will and its pathology could not be seen, it was felt to be due to the limitations of technology, which would be overcome in due time.[4]

Doctors began applying the diseases-of-the-will label to an increasingly broad swath of human behavior. Rush asserted that lying, murder, and thievery were diseases of the will. He intended to "render them the subjects of the kind and lenient hand of medicine."[5]

Rush was the American leader of a related movement known as "moral treatment." This was a new approach in dealing with the mentally ill. Moral treatment advocated humane conditions and spiritual instruction for the insane. They were to be treated with kindness rather than chains. Up to that time, physical abuse and cruelty had been the norm.

Under moral therapy, the insane were to attend religious services, be exposed to fine poetry, enjoy fresh-air walks, and be rewarded when behavior was judged to be upright. Insanity was no longer to be viewed as sin or spiritual failing. It was henceforth a hygiene problem, one that would improve when the afflicted were surrounded by the right physical and intellectual environments. Asylums were to be located in pastoral settings away from the degradations of urban life. Moral treatment also included physical remedies, such as regulated diets, laxatives, and sedatives.

While moral treatment brought needed reforms to the treatment of the mentally ill, it was based on the same faulty assumptions that drove "diseases of the will," namely, that doctors knew more than they really did. The outcome for the mentally ill, though, was positive: they were finally treated with respect. They also had expectations placed on personal conduct, which was, of course, a big part of the respect they were accorded.

The first public expression of the disease model of drunkenness was a call for institutional care for inebriates so that they, like the mentally ill, could receive the benefits of moral treatment. Samuel B. Woodward, the superintendent of the Worcester State Lunatic Asylum, pushed asylum care for inebriates in a series of articles in 1833. After working with the insane, he felt that most drunkards would have their diseased appetites "radically" cured through institutional care and would be able to reenter society as healthy, safe, and temperate men.[6]

In the 1850s, "inebriate homes" were established in major cities. These were privately run small institutions that stressed religious instruction and medical treatment. The Washingtonian Home of Chicago, for instance, employed Nathan S. Davis, who later would become one of the founders of the American Medical Association.

Inebriate homes eventually were deemed inadequate. By limiting themselves to the treatment of voluntary, motivated, middle-class patients, the homes failed to address society's bigger problem: the "rounders"—the intractable poor drunkards who routinely made the rounds between the courts and jails.[7]

Woodward's dream eventually was realized, and drunkards were committed to insane asylums. This led to an unanticipated outcome: rampant disorder. Thomas Kirkbride, superintendent of the Institute of the Pennsylvania Hospital, said that inebriates were recalcitrant and an obstacle to institutional order.[8] Another superintendent noted that as soon as dipsomaniacs sobered up, they became sane and started looking for lawyers.[9] Superintendents became "policeman trying to maintain order" among inebriates who were populating the asylums.[10]

It was natural, then, for superintendents to call for separate asylums. Toward this end, sixteen men organized the American Association for the Cure of Inebriates in 1870. Besides calling for states to support inebriate asylums, they declared that intemperance was an illness caused by an inherited or acquired constitutional susceptibility to "the alcoholic impression" and could be cured through proper treatment.[11] Within the American Medical Association's Public Hygiene and State Medicine section, there were also calls for special institutions for the treatment of inebriety.[12]

The first such institution was the New York State Inebriate Asylum, which opened in Binghamton in 1864. A journalist from *The Atlantic Monthly* magazine visited the asylum early in its fifteen-year history and noted that visitors "see nothing to destroy the impression that the building is a very liberally arranged summer hotel. . . . It is a place [where drunkards] can pause and reflect, and gather strength and knowledge for the final victorious struggle with themselves."[13] He also observed,

> Patients occasionally arrive at the Asylum who expect to be treated in some such way; and when a day or two passes without anything extraordinary or disagreeable happening, they inquire, with visible apprehension, "When the treatment is going to begin." In this sense of the word, there is no treatment here. . . . This Asylum simply gives its inmates rest,

regimen, amusement, society, information. It tries to restore the health and renew the will, and both by rational means.[14]

The New York Asylum eventually closed because of widespread financial mismanagement and fraud and later was converted to house the mentally ill.[15] Governor Lucius Robinson characterized the asylum as a "hotel for the entertainment of wealthy inebriates."[16]

Another large state institution was the Massachusetts Hospital for Dipsomaniacs and Inebriates at Foxborough, which opened in 1893. Cost overruns led it to start admitting the chronically insane by 1905. In 1907, there was a series of reports regarding patient abuse, mismanagement, and graft.[17] A state investigation ended with the dismissal of all hospital officers.

By 1910, the trustees of Foxborough opined that institutionalization would not end drunkenness. Instead, they called for healthy homes, more recreation centers, and schools that prepared people for jobs while also instilling character.[18] It would be hard to conceive this statement as an endorsement of medical treatment for drunkenness.

Against this background of struggling institutional care, there arose several popular entrepreneurial treatments. One became known as the "The Keeley Cure." Its founder, Leslie Keeley, a former Civil War surgeon, boldly declared in 1879 that "drunkenness is a disease and I can cure it." His treatment consisted of four shots per day of a proprietary compound (which was later found to be bichloride of gold) and twice-daily individualized tonics. Keeley relied heavily on appeals to masculinity and camaraderie. The *Chicago Tribune*, referring to the "Cure," noted that drunkards "went away sots and returned gentlemen." The 1893 World's Fair in Chicago hosted a "Keeley Day." Over half a million alcoholics took the "cure" between 1880 and 1920. Keeley claimed a 95 percent success rate. At its peak, there were 118 Keeley Institutes throughout the country.[19]

The "cure" received mixed reviews from the medical establishment, which generally considered Keeley an entrepreneurial quack. On the other hand, Keeley was helping to promote the disease model, which was not widely accepted by the public. Over time, it became clear that a high percentage of those "cured" had relapsed. *Time* magazine noted in a postmortem that at least part of Keeley's success owed to "excitingly confessional sermons to female temperance societies."[20]

Another entrepreneurial treatment was the "Towns-Lambert Cure." Charles B. Towns, a New York City entrepreneur, opened a hospital for drunkards and opiate addicts in 1901. He catered largely to the rich and famous. His "cure" consisted of inducing delirium with hallucinogens, then purging the gastrointestinal tract before restoring health with physical therapy, massages, and exercise. Towns courted the medical profession. His partner, Dr. Alexander Lambert, was the personal physician of Theodore Roosevelt. Towns claimed 75 to 95 percent success, but Lambert placed it at a still-respectable 25 percent.[21] Interestingly, Bill Wilson, one of the founders of Alcoholics Anonymous, entered this hospital four times between 1928 and 1934. He appears to have formed some of the guiding principles of Alcoholics Anonymous during an episode of delirium.

HEREDITY

Like the modern disease model, an important feature of the early model was the claim that alcoholism was a genetic disorder. While this argument bolstered the scientific credentials of the model, it also helped lead to its demise.

The genetic component of the early disease model was called "hereditary degeneration," which was the theory that alcohol caused damage to germ cells, thereby affecting subsequent generations. An 1834 report to the House of Commons during Britain's gin epidemic claimed that alcohol threatened to bring about "the diminution of the physical power and longevity of a large part of the British population . . . by such habits one generation after another becomes more and more effeminate, till they scarcely deserve the name of human beings."[22]

Bénédict Augustin Morel (1809–1873) was a French psychiatrist and the intellectual force behind degeneration. He believed that alcoholism culminated in the ultimate extinction of afflicted families through sterile imbecility and idiocy.

The application of the term "degeneracy," however, was selective. The inebriety of the upper classes was thought to be caused by a nervous constitution. Only the inebriety of the working classes was felt to be due to degeneration. Hereditary degeneration was not thought to affect aboriginals or Africans, who were believed to have the mental and moral prowess of children. Degeneration implied an earlier sophisticated state that was not thought to be characteristic of these groups.[23]

The belief that inebriety was inherited was frequently touted in the popular press. An October 18, 1891, *New York Times* article claimed that "by far the largest proportion of the victims of alcohol are born with seeds of the disease in the very fibre of their physical constitutions . . . the best medical experts . . . declare that 60 per cent of their patients are born with hereditary physical conditions which require only some exciting cause to burst into the drink disease." Temperance literature frequently recited the inheritance line.

The theory of degeneracy was associated with the increasing use of coercion. Advocates of nineteenth-century inebriate asylums promoted a system of controls that emphasized indeterminate detention for the degenerate, lower classes, and shorter-term remedial treatment for the upper and middle classes.[24]

The theory of degeneracy ultimately led to the eugenics movement. Concern about alcohol moved from a concern about its effect on individuals and their families to fears about its effect on the entire white race. The threat of alcohol was shifted from germ poison to race poison.[25]

American physician Robert Fleming visited Germany in 1936 where he noted "for all practical purposes [the Germans have] only one therapeutic approach to severe chronic alcoholism . . . the surgical approach—sterilization."[26] Once alcoholics were thought to "scarcely deserve the name of human beings," it was easy to take it to the next level, which was to mark them for extermination, as eventually happened in Nazi Germany.

When the early disease model hooked up with the eugenics movement, it began to fall off the map. Its demise, though, also had other influences. Professor MacLeod has suggested that by adopting a view of inebriety as inherited rather than environmentally caused, proponents of the model cut themselves off from the burgeoning public health movement.[27] But the model also died in large part because of prohibition. States were not willing to fund dubious efforts with treatment when the definitive solution seemed at hand. As one temperance leader put it, "Women believe in prevention rather than cure . . . we think it is better to turn off the spigot than to mop up the floor."[28]

2

DEMON RUM

Before alcohol became a problem, Americans were heavy drinkers. In colonial times, per capita intake was about seven gallons of pure alcohol each year, which is roughly three times the average consumption today. But as cities began to grow, their problems multiplied, and the Protestant faithful began to look around for causes. Perhaps influenced by the emerging "diseases-of-the-will" philosophy, it was natural to assume that something was corrupting the human will, and alcohol became suspect.

THE TEMPERANCE MOVEMENT

The theological justification for temperance was that the body is the temple of the Holy Spirit.[1] Consuming anything harmful was considered a spiritual violation. That alcohol was harmful was taken as a fundamental principle of the temperance movement. Renowned preacher Lyman Beecher (1775–1863) laid out the case for temperance with the publication of his *Six Sermons*. He called intemperance a "national sin." As did Dr. Benjamin Rush, he likened intemperance to a physical disease: "I know that much is said about the prudent use of ardent spirits; but we might as well speak of the prudent use of the plague."[2]

Temperance leaders often took their cues from the medical profession. The National Temperance Society claimed that "drunkenness [is] a sin and a disease—a sin first, then a disease."[3]

Most nineteenth-century physicians supported the temperance movement. Dr. William B. Carpenter, renowned surgeon and naturalist, wrote in 1861,

Of all the causes which are at present conspiring to degrade the physical, moral, and intellectual condition of the mass of the people, there is not one to be compared in potency with the abuse of alcoholic liquors. . . . Every one who wishes well to his kind, therefore, must be interested in the inquiry how this monster-evil can be best eradicated.[4]

The temperance movement was the most popular social cause of the 1800s, even more popular than the drive to abolish slavery. By 1837, it was estimated that one-third of the population of New York City was actively involved in a temperance cause.

Temperance ideology initially advocated moderation—hence its name. It urged abstinence from spirits but not from beer, cider, or wine, which were not thought to be as harmful. Temperance pledges were popular at the time and were initially aimed at hard liquor.

The early temperance movement focused on the repentant drinker. The Washingtonian Society, a precursor to Alcoholics Anonymous, relied on public confession and storytelling about drunken debaucheries—the more detailed, the more popular. The growth of temperance organizations was fueled by the model of evangelical revivalism.[5] It was believed that chronic drunkards could turn their lives around with the right amount of enlightened spirituality.

Temperance ideology underwent several changes during the nineteenth century. The first was that calls for moderation were soon replaced by calls for abstinence. Not only were pledges and moral persuasion failing to instill moderation, but it was becoming increasingly obvious that many people were getting drunk from beer, wine, and cider. In later editions of his *Treatise*, Benjamin Rush removed references advocating the use of these beverages.

Calls for abstinence were soon replaced by calls for legal prohibition. Toward the middle of the nineteenth century, it was clear that admonishment and dire warnings were not bringing the necessary social change. Saloons were becoming centers of vice and corruption. Legal prohibition was felt to be the only rational means to control the problem.

The first state to legally prohibit alcohol was Maine in 1851. It allowed alcohol only for medicinal, mechanical, or manufacturing purposes. The prohibition sentiment rapidly spread, and by 1855, twelve states had joined Maine.

The shift from moderation to abstinence to prohibition correlated with a shift in how the movement viewed personal responsibility. When drunkards did not respond to calls for moderation or abstinence, temperance reformers began to view inebriates as *unable* to control themselves. "Demon rum" became the problem, not the drunkard. Moderate drinkers began to receive more scorn than drunkards. As one temperance tract put it, "If there be any difference in the degrees of guilt . . . the moderate drinker is worse than the drunkard."[6] Those who were not yet overtaken were assumed to know better than to head down that path.

Along the way, temperance reformers encountered a formidable opponent: human nature. People found ways to lawfully skirt prohibition laws. Maine's law, for instance, stipulated that it was unlawful to sell alcohol. Saloon keepers instead sold crackers for five cents and supplied a free drink with each cracker. Some establishments sold tickets to watch "blind pigs." Each ticket came with a free drink.[7]

The Women's Christian Temperance Union (WCTU) began to view saloons as the problem. They conducted prayer vigils outside of them, encouraging owners to close shop and sign pledges to never sell alcohol again. Those vigils sometimes turned violent, as when the hatchet-wielding Carrie Nation rode into Kansas towns to oversee the closing of local saloons. Several Ohio towns passed ordinances prohibiting WCTU marches for fear of violence.

THE ERA OF PROHIBITION

The Eighteenth Amendment outlawing the sale of alcohol was ratified in 1919 to little fanfare. Support for its passage came from many corners: anti-German sentiment during World War I and the fact that the country had already largely been dry. Thirty-three states had passed prohibition laws, most of which were justified as wartime sacrifices. But there had also been aggressive and smart politicking by the Anti-Saloon League, which had gained the support of influential industrialists like John D. Rockefeller Jr. He felt that industrial output would be enhanced when the masses could no longer drink.

The Eighteenth Amendment stated the following: "The manufacture, sale, or transportation of intoxicating liquors within, the importation thereof into, or the exportation thereof from the United States and all territory subject to the jurisdiction thereof for beverage purposes is hereby prohibited." Like Maine's law, it did not forbid the consumption of alcohol. Thus, as Professor Norman Clark has pointed out, the Yale Club of New York had the resources and foresight to store fifteen years' worth of quality liquor for the benefit of its private members.[8]

The predicted benefits of prohibition flowed as freely as the liquor. Will Rogers is noted to have said that "prohibition is better than no liquor at all." On the eve of enactment of the Eighteenth Amendment, the Reverend Billy Sunday stirred audiences with this declaration:

> The reign of tears is over. The slums will soon be a memory. We will turn our prisons into factories and our jails into storehouses and corncribs. Men will walk upright now, women will smile and children will laugh. Hell will be forever for rent.[9]

These benefits, however, never materialized. During prohibition, New York City Mayor Fiorello La Guardia said, "It would take a police force of 250,000 to enforce the Prohibition Act, and another 200,000 to police the police." Al Capone estimated that payoffs to policemen and to other public officials ran to $30 million each year, which was roughly half his profits.[10] Another famous bootlegger, George Remus, paid $20 million per year to pay off corrupt politicians.[11] In 1926, Mayor William E. Dever of Chicago admitted to Congress that 60 percent of his police force was in the liquor business and that he could do nothing about it.[12] In Texas, just months after prohibition began, a liquor still was found on the farm of Senator Morris Sheppard, who was one of the Eighteenth Amendment's chief backers in Congress. The Federal Bureau of Prohibition had to be reorganized to reduce corruption. Commissioner Henry Anderson concluded that "the fruitless efforts at enforcement are creating public disregard not only for this law but for all laws."[13]

Prohibition may actually have increased intemperance by increasing the availability of alcohol. In most cities, there were twice as many speakeasies as saloons closed by prohibition. According to a CATO report,[14] annual per capita consumption and the percentage of per capita income spent on alcohol had been steadily falling before prohibition, but both increased during prohibition, and this had the unintended consequence of making it "cool" to drink. One historian noted, "To be served alcohol in restaurants required displays of wit and humor; to know where the best speakeasies were demanded entry into exclusive realms . . . to New York sophisticates, the decade became a blur of cocktails, cabarets, and . . . beautiful jazz babies."[15]

Public opinion gradually turned against prohibition. John D. Rockefeller Jr. wrote a letter[16] to the *New York Times* that became extremely influential in turning the tide. The Rockefellers had long supported prohibition through hefty donations to the Anti-Saloon League. But in his letter, Rockefeller admitted,

> Drinking has generally increased; that the speakeasy has replaced the saloon, not only unit for unit, but probably two-fold if not three-fold; that a vast array of lawbreakers has been recruited and financed on a colossal scale; that many of our best citizens, piqued at what they regarded as an infringement of their private rights, have openly and unabashedly disregarded the Eighteenth Amendment; that as an inevitable result respect for all law has been greatly lessened; that crime has increased to an unprecedented degree—I have slowly and reluctantly come to believe.

In retrospect, it is clear that temperance leaders misjudged the problem of inebriety—or at least its manageability. Those who wanted to drink found ways to do so. The WCTU and other temperance organizations supported the disease model only when it appeared that state or local prohibition efforts were failing.[17] But clearly, the disease model of the nineteenth century never reached its critical mass of popularity, as it took a back seat to the drive for prohibition.

Sociologist Joseph Gusfield, in a widely read article,[18] argued that laws have either instrumental (enforced) or symbolic (unenforced) effects and that prohibition functioned more as a symbolic law. It had become a value-based dividing line between Protestant and Catholic, rural and urban, native and immigrant, and middle class and lower class. Whether legislation was passed or defeated was a symbolic expression of which group had power. Legal prohibition represented the symbolic dominance of rural, Protestant, white, middle-class values. According to Gusfield, even though the law was widely broken, "it was clear whose law it was."

3

DISEASE CRUSADERS

The repeal of prohibition in 1933 meant that the greatest social movement of the nineteenth century had failed. It also meant that there was no consensus about what to do next. Repeal had shifted control of alcohol to the individual states, where each would set its own laws regarding sales and transport. Even though many now agreed on the shortcomings of national prohibition, "wet" and "dry" sentiments were still very much at war.

For instance, in 1936, the Medical College of Virginia was asked by the state legislature to prepare a scientific report on alcohol and its effects on the body. The report, which was published in 1938, concluded that the moderate use of alcohol "does not shorten the life span and probably plays no important part in the perpetration of lawlessness." The report indicated that alcohol helped digestion, gave bibbers a "lift," and produced "a feeling of self-satisfaction and physical well-being."

The report generated widespread opposition. *Time* magazine noted that the legislative representative of the Women's Christian Temperance Union had "cried in horror: 'The book does not refer to alcohol as a poison.'" The legislature subsequently banned the report and ordered all copies to be burned.[1]

It was in this setting that seven individuals—six of whom had severe alcohol problems—pieced together the modern disease model. They were Bill W., Dr. Bob, E. M. Jellinek, Mrs. Marty Mann, R. Brinkley Smithers, Thomas Pike, and Senator Harold Hughes. Each contributed to shifting the alcohol issue from one of "universal poison" or "demon rum" to a problem that affected only a small proportion of the population—those who would come to be known as "alcoholics."

BILL W. AND DR. BOB

Mr. Bill Wilson and Dr. Bob Smith founded Alcoholics Anonymous (AA) in 1935. Both had been severe alcoholics. On a business trip to Akron, Ohio, in 1935, Wilson felt an urge to drink but wanted to stay sober, so he sought help from former drinkers. There he met Smith, a practicing physician. They developed a word-of-mouth, self-help program that was based on admitting powerlessness over alcohol, asking for help from a higher power, making amends, and taking this message to other alcoholics. In 1937, they published *The Big Book*, which laid out these principles in twelve steps.

The movement grew rapidly and received a boost in membership from a famous March 1, 1941, article in the *Saturday Evening Post*, which almost overnight was said to have doubled AA's membership.

Bill Wilson, possibly drawing on his treatment experiences at the Charles B. Towns Hospital, spoke about his personal conversion in a 1945 lecture at Yale:

> You see, here was my friend talking to me, one alcoholic talking to another. I could no longer say, "he doesn't understand me." Sure he understood me. We had done a lot of drinking together, and gone the same route of humiliation, despair and defeat. Yes, he could understand.
>
> When he had gone away, I fell into a very deep depression, the blackest that I had ever known. And in that depression, I cried out, "If there is a God, will He show Himself?" Then came a sudden experience in which it seemed the room lit up. It felt as though I stood on the top of a mountain, that a great clean wind blew, that I was free. The sublime paradox of strength coming out of weakness.[2]

AA popularized alcoholism as a disease by calling it a physical allergy.[3] This was a metaphor for "loss of control." In practice, AA never gave the disease model much emphasis. Doctors, for example, were expected to refer patients to AA, but it was never the practice of AA to send its members back to doctors for help. The disease metaphor was used mainly to make people feel comfortable about coming forward for help.

It worked. Today there are an estimated 2 million members world-wide, of which 1.2 million reside in the United States. Most drug and alcohol treatment programs are modeled after AA in that they actively employ the twelve steps as the major framework for treatment. More is said about AA in Chapter 7.

E. M. JELLINEK

A man with no formal scientific credentials, "Dr." E. M. Jellinek (1890–1963) became the world's recognized authority on alcoholism. His entry into the alcohol field started when he was hired by a struggling organization named the Research Council on Problems of Alcohol (RCPA), which was formed in 1937 by a group of scientists who were hoping to bring objective science to bear on the emotional hyperbole that still characterized debates about alcohol in the postrepeal era.

The RCPA had difficulty raising money.[4] With a projected budget of $458,700 for its first three years of operation, it raised only $2,191 during its first twelve months, this despite getting front-page coverage in the *New York Times*.[5] The organization finally landed a $25,000 grant from the Carnegie Corporation to organize the world's scientific research literature regarding alcohol and hired Jellinek for the task.

Jellinek's literature work was eventually moved to Yale University's Center of Alcohol Studies, which was studying the physiology and metabolism of alcohol. Yale published—and Jellinek edited—the *Quarterly Journal of Studies on Alcohol*, which at the time was the only American scientific journal devoted to alcohol. The journal facilitated the shift toward alcoholism with advocacy pieces like this from 1942:

> The "alcoholic" is a sick man who is exceptionally reactive to alcohol. To students of inebriety this is practically a banality; but establish this fully in the consciousness of the public and the first step will have been taken toward winning it to the scientific approach to the problem. . . . When these ideas have been fully accepted by a large number of people, the necessary identification has been effected, the crowd has collected, and the "yes" response becomes automatic, uncritical, and on the emotional level. The basic requirements are fulfilled for putting into effect the findings of science by creating definite goals. These findings, originally on the intellectual level, are sterile with the public. They can only fructify into popular action when they are put to crowds in the form of

sentiments. . . . When the dissemination of these ideas is begun through the existing media of public information, press, radio and platform, which will consider them as news, a new public attitude can be shaped. Fortunately, it will not be difficult to use these media . . . for this purpose because, no matter how often the idea may be repeated, it will remain news until its acceptance has become universal.[6]

To further the alcoholism cause, Jellinek organized the Yale Summer School of Alcohol Studies in 1943. This four-week seminar educated social workers, ministers, temperance educators, high school teachers, and college professors. In 1944, the center also opened several Yale Plan Clinics, which were the nation's first outpatient treatment facilities for alcoholism. Patients received psychiatric and medical evaluations and were referred to group therapy, AA meetings, or detoxification in hospitals. In retrospect, there was no body of scientific knowledge that informed the medical treatment of alcoholism, but the Yale doctors did not let that fact deter them.

A July 1950 feature article in *Harper's Magazine* trumpeted an 80 percent success rate for those who underwent treatment at the Yale Plan Clinics.[7] This was highly overstated, of course, but it fit the scientific optimism of the time.

Among Jellinek's many writings was a 1952 paper wherein he divided alcoholism into four phases: "prealcoholic," "prodromal," "crucial," and "chronic."[8] He developed these phases by reviewing mailed-in surveys from ninety-eight members of AA. That is, he based his phases on the opinions of a small group of people who were convinced that they had a chronic disease.[9] According to fellow researcher Robert Straus, Jellinek knew that the sample was "ridiculously biased," but he used it anyway.[10]

In his book *The Disease Concept of Alcoholism*, Jellinek claimed that "there is not one alcoholism, but a whole variety."[11] He defined five different "species" of the disease and named them "alpha," "beta," "gamma," "delta," and "epsilon." He also presented several dozen different theories about alcoholism; some positioned alcoholism as a psychological illness, others that it was only a symptom of psychological illness, and still others that alcoholism was a "physiopathological process."

If you spend time studying Jellinek's numerous "phases," "species," and "theories," it is easy to come away with the feeling that, while he believed strongly in the disease model, as late as 1960 he was still trying to formulate a coherent idea of it. He came close to admitting as much, criticizing researchers who "assert that alcoholism is an illness . . . but take it for granted that this is a well-established fact."[12] This statement came after he had spent years coaxing the World Health Organization into recognizing alcoholism as a disease—which it finally did in 1956—and helping Yale establish treatment facilities and advocating for insurance companies and state governments to pay for the treatment of alcoholism.

Jellinek never earned a university degree,[13] but he was an intelligent and prodigious scientist. In addition to editing the *Quarterly Journal of Studies on Alcohol*, organizing the Yale Plan Clinics, conducting the Summer School of Alcohol Studies, and initiating the Yale Plan for Business and Industry, [14] Jellinek continued to oversee the literature archiving operation. He was also fluent in at least seven languages, which helped when he moved to the World Health Organization in 1951. There, he was able to procure copies of the literature archives and disseminate them to sixteen different countries.[15]

Jellinek's efforts went a long way toward convincing the world that alcoholism was a disease. At the very least, he kept laymen in awe of science. His famous quip, "It comes to this, that a disease is what the medical profession recognizes as such . . . whether a part of the lay public likes it or not,"[16] shows not only the confidence he had in his work but also that he was not above using old-fashioned bullying to push the case.

MRS. MARTY MANN

One of the historians of the disease model has argued that the single most influential person responsible for the social promotion of the disease concept of alcoholism was Mrs. Marty Mann.[17] She was the founder and force behind the National Committee for Education on Alcoholism (NCEA), created and sponsored by the Yale Center in 1944. It became an independent organization in 1950 and changed its name to the National Council on Alcoholism (NCA) in 1956. Today, the group is called the National Council on Alcoholism and Drug Dependence.

Mrs. Marty Mann was beautiful, articulate, intelligent, and full of chutzpah. Her father was a corporate officer with Marshall Field. She had a privileged upbringing and attended finishing school in Florence, Italy. Marty's father would later lose his career and fortune to drinking, leaving three younger children at home without the financial largesse that Marty had enjoyed.

Marty began drinking in her teens and would eventually survive two suicide attempts, numerous hospitalizations, and the demise of her own promising writing career. At the age of thirty-four, she landed at the Blythewood Sanitarium in Greenwich, Connecticut, as a charity case. While continuing her drinking sprees at the hospital (it had an open-campus policy), her psychiatrist, Harry Tiebout, let her review an early manuscript of what would become AA's *Big Book.*

Initially repulsed by the book's frequent references to God, she would go on to have her own road-to-Damascus experience and her story is now part of AA's *Big Book.* It's the chapter titled "Women Suffer Too."

While Marty would have many relapses during her life,[18] she developed a vision for a nationwide grassroots-level education campaign that would promote the disease of alcoholism. She planned to include a push for hospitals and clinics to start diagnosing and treating the disorder. In 1944, she pitched her ideas to the Yale Center, which within days began to sponsor the NCEA with Mann as its executive director. The board consisted of members of the Yale Center, medical doctors, and representatives from the alcohol beverage industry.[19]

Marty's charisma and style garnered lavish press coverage wherever she went. In 1946, the *New York Times Magazine* profiled Mann with a piece titled "The Sick Person We Call an Alcoholic," wherein she argued that the alcoholic "should not be jailed for being drunk; he should be sent to a hospital to be cured."[20]

Yale eventually had issues with the NCEA, not the least of which was that the populism of the new organization was at odds with Yale's staid tradition of scholarship. The NCEA was also competing for donations with the Yale Center.[21] The NCEA was forced to leave Yale in 1949, prompting a period of severe financial hardship. Its struggles would be short lived. When the press announced the group's financial problems, a new benefactor arrived on the scene.

R. BRINKLEY SMITHERS

By the early 1950s, the NCEA had affiliates in more than fifty communities in twenty-seven states. In 1954, a forty-seven-year-old alcoholic who was then a patient[22] at the Charles B. Towns Hospital in New York read about the NCEA and decided to solve its financial woes.[23] He was R. Brinkley Smithers, heir of an IBM fortune.

Smithers personally contributed over $25 million to the NCEA and other organizations that promoted the disease of alcoholism. He awarded grant money through the Christopher D. Smithers Foundation, named for his father. The foundation gave $10 million to the Roosevelt Hospital in New York City in 1971 to establish the Smithers Alcoholism Treatment and Training Center. Smithers underwrote E. M. Jellinek's influential 1960 book *The Disease Concept of Alcoholism*. Smithers also funded—with the help of the federal government—the move of the Center of Alcohol Studies from Yale to Rutgers in 1962.

THOMAS P. PIKE

Pike inherited a successful family oil-drilling business. He had a habit of leaving his wife and young children at home to go on prolonged drinking binges.[24] He would live in bars and hotels and afterward would experience "the tortuous pain of my own shame and unrelieved guilt." He eventually became sober in 1946 through AA and a conversion to the Catholic faith. Later in life, he would have severe psychiatric problems, resulting in suicide attempts and electroshock treatments.

His success in the business community led him to be nominated and confirmed as assistant secretary of defense in 1954 under President Eisenhower. By 1960, he was president of the Stanford Board of Trustees. He was a close friend and confidant of Richard Nixon and was the California chairman for his presidential campaigns. He was also a board member of the NCA and the RAND Corporation. He resigned from RAND in 1976 after it published research supporting controlled-drinking outcomes, which were theoretically at odds with the disease model. Pike's major contributions to the disease model stemmed from his work at the NCA from 1965 to 1978 and his friendship and influence with President Nixon (addressed below).

SENATOR HAROLD HUGHES
AND THE FEDERAL GOVERNMENT

Against this backdrop of dedicated individuals, private philanthropists, and the support of the news media, there was a drive for the federal government to take the lead in pushing the disease model. If successful, not only would the alcoholism movement have a new source of funding, but it would gain substantial legitimacy in the process.

The key player pushing federal legislation was another former alcoholic, Senator Harold Hughes of Iowa. Hughes was the first member of Congress to publicly proclaim that he was an alcoholic. His personal history was marked by numerous arrests for drunkenness. In 1946, his wife had petitioned the Ada County (Iowa) Sanity Commission to have him committed to the state asylum for inebriates. Later, during an aborted suicide attempt, he had a spiritual epiphany that turned him toward God and AA.

Hughes served as governor of Iowa from 1962 to 1968. He won a U.S. Senate seat in 1968. During the summer of 1969, he chaired the Special Subcommittee on Alcoholism and Narcotics, which held hearings across the country. Marty Mann, Bill W., religious leaders, scientists, and numerous Hollywood celebrities testified about their alcoholism. In 1970, Hughes introduced the Comprehensive Alcohol Abuse and Alcoholism Prevention, Treatment, and Rehabilitation Act, which came to bear his name. President Nixon, however, did not support the act, and his advisers recommended that he veto it. But in late December 1970, a group of prominent former alcoholics and friends of Nixon persuaded him to sign the legislation. This group included Thomas Pike, R. Brinkley Smithers, Donald Kendall of Pepsi-Cola, and James S. Kemper of Kemper Insurance. Pike referred to the legislation as alcoholism's Magna Carta.[25]

The Hughes Act created the National Institute on Alcohol Abuse and Alcoholism and provided block grants to states that set up addiction treatment centers throughout the country. Subsequent legislation in 1972 established the institute's sister organization, the National Institute on Drug Abuse.

THE REST OF THE STORY

The loudest voices pushing the disease model were not medical scientists but rather members of AA. Yet neither Bill Wilson, Bob Smith, Marty Mann, R. Brinkley Smithers, Thomas Pike, nor Harold Hughes obtained their sobriety through medical treatment. They all became sober through AA, and they all had spiritual experiences as part of their conversions. So why did they feel the need to medicalize their journeys?

The avowed reason was that if drunkards believed that they had an illness, they would be more willing to come forward and seek help. But there may have been less obvious dynamics at work. All these individuals had deeply troubled lives. Mann survived two suicide attempts and was a frequent patient of psychiatric asylums. R. Brinkley Smithers had fifty or more hospitalizations for drunkenness. Thomas Pike left his family to pursue forays on skid row. Senator Hughes was in and out of jail and almost ended his life holding a gun in the bathtub. Bill Wilson squandered a small fortune and his Wall Street career on drink. These were embarrassing segments of their lives, and it is possible that each carried some degree of shame and guilt.

Clearly, becoming sober and productive citizens—as they all did—should have been proof enough of individual redemption. But these were not normal people. They were highly motivated and successful and had large public identities. Some might argue that they also had large egos. There was only one thing that could remove whatever shame they still carried with them: a disease of the will. If drunkenness was a brain disease, then they were not responsible for anything they did while drinking. Thus, with each public pronouncement that alcoholism was a disease, they positioned themselves as enlightened followers of science while disavowing personal responsibility for their behavior.

Paradoxically, the disease model plays next to no role inside AA. In fact, the key features of the twelve-step program—developing faith in a higher power, taking a moral inventory, reversing character defects, admitting mistakes, and making amends—are specifically tailored to deal with guilt and shame. AA seems to have accepted these painful emotions even if some of its more prominent members did not.

Whatever personal agendas may have been at work, the drive for medicalization resulted in profound changes in the cultural landscape. The disease model and an extensive treatment network were established when little was known about what was going on in the brain and still less was known about what, if anything, doctors could do about it.

And many in the medical community remained skeptical late into the game. When Thomas Pike and his wife endowed a medical school professorship at the University of California, Los Angeles, in 1978, they noted that there was a lot of ignorance among doctors and the entire medical community.[26] Interestingly, they were trying to educate doctors about the disease model, not about AA.

Another force behind the disease model was the alcohol beverage industry. After the RCPA hired Jellinek and spent the Carnegie grant money, its financial woes continued. The federal government was not supporting work in the alcohol field, and at that time the only offers for support came from the liquor industry. The RCPA initially refused to accept "wet" money so as not to be seen as a biased organization. But eventually it had no choice. Karl Bowman, who at that time was chair of the RCPA's Executive Committee, in the end accepted money from a group of distillers who had come forward. The focus of RCPA work subsequently changed and began to focus only on the study of the *disease of alcoholism.* Sociologist Ron Roizen has termed this "Bowman's Compromise."[27]

This was not the only path that alcohol research could have taken. There was still plenty of work yet to be done regarding alcohol's effects on the body, the physiological metabolism of alcohol, public safety issues, how education might affect consumption rates, and what kind of regulatory controls might minimize abusive drinking habits.

As it happened, the shift toward alcoholism as a disease benefited the liquor industry. After the repeal of prohibition, it was increasingly recognized that most people who drank did not develop "loss of control." Clearly, alcohol was not a universal poison, but there was a percentage of the population—about 5 to 10 percent—who seemed to drink too much and who developed complications. It was in the liquor industry's interest to support research and policies focusing on this group. At the very least, the industry would be seen supporting what was considered cutting-edge science. A more self-serving reason, however, was that if alcoholism was a disease, then roughly 90 to 95 percent of people could consume alcohol and not worry about becoming addicted.

The shift toward alcoholism also worked for the "dry" forces who had finally found a postrepeal niche that everyone respected. Alcohol really was poison—and the temperance message really was valid—albeit for a small percentage of the population.

Roizen has pointed out, however, that there is no evidence the liquor industry influenced the RCPA toward this "problem-in-the-man-and-not-in-the-bottle formulation."[28] Correspondence between Karl Bowman and other members of the RCPA indicate that this was an internal decision. It was about the only area where scientific research could go and not be seen as being influenced by either "wet" or "dry" forces. It was neutral territory, as it had not been part of the rancorous temperance debates.

CONCLUSION

The modern disease model of alcoholism was successful because it appealed to so many constituencies and provided an answer to the alcohol problem in postprohibition America. The model subsequently was expanded to explain drug abuse and other compulsive behaviors, such as gambling, overeating, shopping, and sex.

The next chapter examines drug prohibition laws, which today provide important tactical support for the disease model: if drug abuse is a disease, then drugs are pathogens and must be banned. The origins of prohibition laws, however, are more ignominious.

4

RACISM, PROGRESSIVISM, AND DRUG LAWS

Prohibition laws are relatively recent phenomena, dating only to the late nineteenth and early twentieth centuries. There have been a few exceptions. During the Inquisition, opium was outlawed by the Roman Catholic Church because anything from the Orient was considered diabolical. Islamic law has generally outlawed all drug use unless it was done for therapeutic reasons.

For most of recorded history, though, alcohol, cocaine, opium, and marijuana have been consumed freely and legally. Earlier societies confronted the problem of substance abuse, but prohibition laws were seldom felt to be useful. The historical approach was to allow intoxicating substances to be consumed but to punish any use that brought harm to society.

Chinese texts from 1100 BC, for instance, addressed alcoholic beverages and noted that "men will not do without. To prohibit them and secure a total abstinence from them is beyond the power even of sages. Here, therefore, we have warnings of the abuse of them."[1] The Chinese "Shoo-King" texts sanctioned drinking but in moderation: "When you have largely done your duty in ministering to your aged and serving your sovereign, you may eat and drink freely and to satiety."[2] Chinese rulers issued guidance on the proper use of fermented drinks, which they often tied to religious festivals, but placed harsh sanctions on habitual drunkenness up to and including the threat of death.

In ancient Greece, both Plato and Xenophon praised the moderate use of wine as healthy but condemned drunkenness. In 594 BC, the Greeks ordered the death penalty for drunken magistrates.[3]

Early Christians held similar views. St. Paul praised the use of wine,[4] especially for medicinal purposes,[5] but consistently condemned drunkenness.[6] The ancients appeared to understand that self-indulgence was entirely normal, and often there were no sanctions whatsoever against its abuse. The legal code of Hammurabi (ca. 1750 BC), for instance, contains the entire criminal and civil code for ancient Babylon. It does not mention any sanctions against alcohol misuse or drunkenness even though alcohol consumption was widespread.

During the Middle Ages, beer and wine making were the purview of the monasteries with sanctions only on its misuse. St. Gildas the Wise (AD 570) wrote, "If any one (that is, a monk) through drinking too freely gets thick of speech, so that he cannot join in the psalmody, he is to be deprived of his supper."[7] Alcoholic beverages were the only foodstuffs allowed during times of fasting at the monasteries.

Statutory sanctions in colonial America were limited to the misuse of alcohol. In 1675, the New Jersey assembly imposed a fine of one shilling for the first act of drunkenness, two shillings for the second, and six pence for the third and every succeeding offense. Sometimes drunks were placed into the stocks but not because they were intoxicated—almost everyone drank on a regular basis—but only when being drunk disturbed the peace.[8]

OPIUM

Opium and cocaine have tended to have closer ties to the medical profession; they have been generally regarded as medicinal agents. Ancient Egyptian medical texts, for instance, record the use of opium for both pain control and crying children. Homer (850 BC) writes about the drug's intoxicating, pain-relieving, and sleep-inducing properties in *The Iliad* and *The Odyssey*. It was known as nepenthe, which means "chasing away sorrows." Hippocrates (460–377 BC) wrote of the calming properties of opium wine.[9] Shortly thereafter, Alexander the Great introduced opium to Persia and India, and around AD 400, Arab traders introduced the drug to China.

During the Middle Ages, Islamic physicians prescribed opium for anesthesia and melancholy. After the Inquisition, opium was reintroduced into Europe by the pharmacist Paracelsus in a mixture that contained citrus juice and gold. It was called "laudanum," and a form of it is still available by prescription.

In the 1700s, Chinese emperors began to prohibit the domestic use of opium because of trade imbalances with European countries. This ultimately led to two Opium Wars between China and the British Empire in the 1800s, which led to further opium exports to China as the defeated country.

Nineteenth-century Americans imported and consumed large amounts of opium. Per capita consumption, in grams of crude opium per annum, rose from twelve in the 1840s to fifty-two in the 1890s. While some of this was used recreationally, it was more commonly used to treat ailments—real or imagined. After the invention of the hypodermic syringe in the 1850s, morphine began to be used for surgical procedures and chronic pain.

The medical profession widely embraced opium because in the nineteenth century most diseases were mysterious and very few effective medicines available.[10] Opium, by contrast, really works. It is extremely effective for both pain and anxiety. Doctors recommended it for almost every known malady.[11] While opium was legal to buy without a prescription, most people got started through the advice of their physicians. Oliver Wendell Holmes Sr., dean of Harvard Medical School in the early 1850s, blamed the medical community for contributing to opium's popularity.[12]

COCAINE

Cocaine became popular in Western society in the nineteenth century after Sigmund Freud celebrated its use and wrote scientific papers about the drug. The drug became an official remedy of the Hay Fever Association. It was also considered a cure for opium addiction. It was sold in patent medicines and elixirs for children. And cocaine is still used today as an anesthetic for eye surgery.

Cocaine has also been popular as a nonmedicinal agent. South American Indians, for instance, have consumed it recreationally for over 5,000 years. In America in the late nineteenth century, Parke-Davis marketed cocaine-laced cigarettes, and Sears & Roebuck sold a syringe and small amount of cocaine for $1.50 in its catalog. Coca-Cola, as its name implies, initially contained cocaine. Vin Mariana was a cocaine wine first marketed in 1863.

THE RISE OF DRUG PROHIBITION

Unlike the alcohol problem, initial efforts to control opium and cocaine arose not from concerns about out-of-control use but rather from fears about immigrants and minorities. When Chinese immigrants came to America in the 1800s to work on the railroads, they brought their recreational opium habits with them. San Francisco outlawed Chinese-run opium dens in 1875. The dens were considered "socially polluting" for the Americans who frequented them.[13] The federal government prohibited importation of opium in 1887 but only if imported by the Chinese.[14]

In 1909, Congress passed the first national legislation that restricted opium use within the borders of the United States. The bill was hastily put together for the Shanghai Opium Commission to show China that America was doing something about the international opium trade. American merchants wanted access to markets in China, but the Chinese wanted a sign that the United States was serious about helping them stop the importation of opium.[15] Interestingly, the U.S. legislation outlawed only the importation of opium for smoking. This again was aimed at Chinese immigrants, as Americans were accustomed to ingesting their opium.

Concerns about cocaine arose when it was linked to blacks in the South. An editorial in the *Journal of the American Medical Association* in 1900 warned that blacks were getting addicted to "a new form of vice" by sniffing cocaine. Dr. Christopher Koch of the State Pharmacy Board of Pennsylvania testified before Congress in 1914 that "most of the attacks upon the white women of the South are the direct result of a cocaine-crazed Negro brain."[16] Common lore at the time was that cocaine would allow the black man to rise above his "place" and that "cocaine-crazed" blacks would be unaffected by mere .32-caliber bullets that police officers used. It was for this reason that many southern law enforcement agencies switched to .38-caliber bullets.[17]

The next major legislation was the Harrison Narcotics Act (1914), which was "to provide for the registration of, with collectors of internal revenue, and to impose a special tax on all persons who produce, import, manufacture, compound, deal in, dispense, sell, distribute, or give away opium or coca leaves, their salts, derivatives, or preparations, and for other purposes."[18] The Harrison Act grew out of U.S. obligations from being signatories to the International Hague Opium Convention of 1912, which was the first international drug control treaty.

The Harrison Act was intended to generate revenue for the U.S. Treasury and to keep track of the narcotic trade. Anyone wanting to sell or dispense the drugs had to pay a registration fee and then a transfer tax for each transaction. Physicians were exempt from the transfer tax, as were manufacturers of patent medicines as long as the concentrations of opium and cocaine remained below specified levels.

The act allowed physicians to prescribe narcotics "in the course of his professional practice only," and many physicians registered in order to prescribe the drug to heroin addicts. Most local law enforcement officials, however, were of the opinion that this was not a legitimate medical practice. Police began arresting prescribers, and several cases made their way to the U.S. Supreme Court,[19] which agreed with this restrictive interpretation of the law. Doctors quit prescribing heroin, and addicts were sent scurrying to the black market to obtain their drugs.

The Harrison Act created a large criminal class and began filling the prisons. By 1928, one-third of federal prisoners were Harrison Act violators.[20] When combined with violators of the Volstead Act (alcohol prohibition), the number of federal convicts in 1932 had increased 561 percent from 1919, and the federal prison population had increased 366 percent.[21]

Most temperance-minded progressives supported the Harrison Act. For them, drugs were indistinguishable from alcohol; they were the cause of immoral behavior, and they threatened the social order. Richard P. Hopson of the World Narcotic Defense Association claimed in the 1920s that the "destruction of the world and the future of the human race" depended on successful eradication of narcotics.[22] In the 1930s, as alcohol prohibition was coming to an end, Harry J. Anslinger, who headed the Federal Bureau of Narcotics (FBN), claimed that "addicts have perpetrated some of the most bizarre and fantastic offenses and sex crimes known to police annals."[23]

MARIJUANA

The consumption of marijuana, or cannabis, in the United States followed an influx of Mexican immigrants in the early twentieth century who were fleeing their country's civil war. During the Great Depression, massive unemployment increased public resentment and fear of Mexican immigrants, escalating concerns about the problem of drugs. In testimony before Congress in 1937, Anslinger claimed that marijuana caused white women to have sexual relations with blacks.[24] He also frequently claimed that marijuana use led to insanity and heroin addiction.

William Randolph Hearst published stories about black men using marijuana to corrupt white women. Hearst was concerned that new techniques for processing hemp for paper would supplant his timber-based paper businesses. The DuPont Corporation, which had just patented nylon, helped lead the fight against marijuana because its bottom line was threatened by the growing industrial use of hemp. Andrew Mellon, the U.S. secretary of the treasury and former president of the Mellon Bank, had financed much of DuPont's business activities. He appointed Anslinger to head the FBN in 1930. Anslinger also married Mellon's niece.

Anslinger led a federal assault on the use of marijuana, but he faced a major obstacle: Americans did not believe that Congress had the constitutional authority to prohibit drugs. Such laws were considered to be under the jurisdiction of the states. The Constitution makes allowance for federal prohibition laws but only through amendments, as happened with alcohol prohibition, or to fulfill international treaty obligations.

The drive for a federal response occurred even while the states were establishing drug prohibition laws on their own. By 1931, almost all states had restricted the buying and selling of cocaine and heroin, with exceptions only for the medical profession and for scientific research. State legislatures were heavily influenced by the Uniform Narcotic Drug Laws, which were being pushed by the National Conference of Commissioners on Uniform State Laws. The states adopted almost verbatim the wording suggested by the commissioners, and by 1937, all states had also passed legislation in some way restricting marijuana.

The problem with these state laws, however, is that they were not consistently enforced. This was because the legislation was driven not by local problems with the drugs but by prohibitionists at the federal level. State laws prohibiting drugs passed largely unnoticed by the media, and no state carried out its own independent studies of the drugs that it was prohibiting. The states uncritically accepted the information that was being disseminated by Anslinger and the FBN. For instance, when Virginia passed the Uniform Narcotic Drug Act in 1934, public concern over marijuana, as measured by attention given the topic in the *Richmond Times-Dispatch*, came after the law was passed, not before.[25]

Marijuana was also growing all over the country—along roadsides, in gardens, and in greenhouses. FBN director Anslinger knew that if the federal government were to wage a war against marijuana, it would need an international treaty.

Anslinger traveled to Geneva, Switzerland, in June 1936 to represent the United States at the Conference for the Suppression of the Illicit Traffic in Dangerous Drugs. This was sponsored by the League of Nations, of which the United States was not a member. Anslinger wanted the conference to define marijuana as a "dangerous drug" and thus establish a worldwide ban against its trade. The conference failed to do so, and the United States was the only country not to sign the ensuing treaty.[26]

The FBN's only option at that point was to push legislation that was modeled after the Harrison Act. Congress passed the Marihuana Tax Act in 1937 after Anslinger flooded congressional hearings with lurid, horrific tales of the effects of marijuana use. Like the Harrison Act, it technically did not make marijuana illegal; it simply placed a huge bureaucratic burden—with severe penalties for noncompliance—on anyone who wanted to sell or buy the drug. The act required parties to register with the federal government, pay a transfer fee to the Department of the Treasury for each transaction, and keep meticulous records in triplicate on special forms that would be inspected on demand by government agents. The Marihuana Act effectively became a prohibition law because absolute compliance with the law was difficult and not worth the costs. For instance, while the registration fee to become a distributor was small (about one dollar), the penalties for any paperwork violation were "not more than $2,000 or imprisoned not more than five years, or both, in the discretion of the court."[27] After passage of the Marihuana Tax Act, Anslinger and the FBN used the transfer tax to suppress the fledgling hemp industry. Interestingly, when the nation entered World War II and needed hemp for ropes, the federal government reversed course. The Department of Agriculture contracted out 350,000 acres of hemp production and created a film titled *Hemp for Victory*, wherein it instructed farmers how to grow and harvest the crop. All this was placed under the supervision of the War Hemp Industries Board.

After the war, the FBN used the 1937 act to go after hemp producers, and by the 1950s there was essentially no hemp industry left in the country.

TIGHTENING THE SCREWS

By the late 1940s, there was growing concern about heroin use by inner-city youths. In 1951, Congress responded by passing the Boggs Act, which established harsh minimum sentences for illegal possession or delivery of drugs—that is, any possession or delivery that was not in accordance with the Harrison Act or Marihuana Tax Act. First convictions for illegal possession of heroin, cocaine, or cannabis carried a mandatory sentence of two to five years in prison. A second offense mandated a five- to ten-year sentence, and a third offense mandated ten to fifteen years. In 1956, the Narcotics Control Act increased even further these mandatory minimum penalties. It also forbade judges from suspending sentences or imposing probation in cases where they felt a prison sentence was inappropriate, and it allowed the death penalty for the distribution of narcotics to minors.

This increasing punitive approach fit the anxieties of the times—the Red Scare, fear of nuclear war, and ongoing antipathy toward minorities, who were still the popular face of the drug problem. Drug use had not yet been embraced by the white youth culture as it would be in the 1960s.

When white youth became the face of the drug culture, federal and state governments had a mixed response. The federal government emphasized a public health and treatment approach for youthful drug users (see below). Governor Nelson Rockefeller of New York, on the other hand, wanted stiffer penalties. The "Rockefeller Drug Laws," signed in 1973, assigned minimum sentences of fifteen years to life in prison for selling as little as two ounces of narcotics or possessing four ounces of the same. In 1979, Governor Hugh Carey repealed these stiff sentences but only for marijuana.

The punitive approach, though, was beginning to unravel. In 1965, Harvard clinical professor Timothy Leary, best known for his advocacy of LSD, was arrested on the Texas–Mexico border and was convicted of two charges related to the possession of marijuana. After receiving a thirty-year sentence, he appealed his conviction all the way to the U.S.

Supreme Court. In *Leary v. United States* (395 U.S. 6), the Court ruled in 1969 that the Marihuana Tax Act was unconstitutional because it deprived Leary of his constitutional right to be free of self-incrimination. Had he registered under the act to be a transferee of marijuana, the Court wrote, he "would surely prove a significant link in a chain of evidence tending to establish his guilt under the state marihuana laws then in effect."

SECURING A FEDERAL RESPONSE

Prohibitionists like Anslinger were dyed-in-the-wool progressives. They were devoted to the idea that cleverly crafted laws could keep people from behaving in unhealthy ways. This mind-set reaches its apotheosis on the world stage. It is also where federal drug warriors knew they had to go to cement federal prohibition.

The League of Nations had been writing drug treaties for its members since its founding in 1920. It had established the World Health Organization and the Permanent Central Opium Board to monitor drug traffic around the world and to advise countries on how to coordinate antidrug efforts. These functions were directly absorbed by the United Nations when the League of Nations dissolved in 1946.

The first major drug control treaty after the 1912 Hague Opium Convention, to which the United States was a signatory, was the 1961 Single Convention on Narcotic Drugs. The United Nations started work on the convention in 1949, but it took twelve years to produce the final product. The convention criminalized possession, not just transfers, of banned substances. Signatories now had the backing of the international community to wage an all-out drug war.

The UN treaty was enacted into law through the Controlled Substance Act (CSA) passed by Congress in 1970. The CSA is Title II of the Comprehensive Drug Abuse Prevention and Control, which also established the five schedules used today to classify controlled drugs. The CSA has been amended several times over the years, mostly in response to other UN treaties that expanded the reach of the Single Convention.

Perhaps the best that can be said about this UN treaty is that it forced the federal government to abandon race-baiting as a basis for the drug war. The Single Convention was a paragon of progressive legislation: it shifted the focus onto health concerns. The preamble to the convention reveals the therapeutic intent of this treaty: "The Parties [are] Concerned with the health and welfare of mankind . . . [and acknowledge] the competence of the United Nations in the field of narcotics control."[28]

The treaty was committed to the disease model of substance abuse, which should not be surprising since E. M. Jellinek was a prominent consultant to the World Health Organization when the treaty was being written. In Article 38, "Measures Against the Abuse of Drugs," we read as follows:

1. The Parties shall give special attention to and take all practicable measures for the prevention of abuse of drugs and for the early identification, treatment, education, after-care, rehabilitation and social reintegration of the persons involved and shall co-ordinate their efforts to these ends.
    2. The Parties shall as far as possible promote the training of personnel in the treatment, after-care, rehabilitation and social reintegration of abusers of drugs.
    3. The Parties shall take all practicable measures to assist persons whose work so requires to gain an understanding of the problems of abuse of drugs and of its prevention, and shall also promote such understanding among the general public if there is a risk that abuse of drugs will become widespread.

While the convention allows for the punishment of traffickers,[29] the therapeutic mantle is never far behind:

The Parties may provide, either as an alternative to conviction or punishment or in addition to conviction or punishment, that such [offenders who are] abusers shall undergo measures of treatment, education, after-care, rehabilitation and social reintegration.[30]

Immediately after the Single Convention became federal law in 1970, there were efforts to trim its wings. Part of the CSA established the National Commission on Marijuana and Drug Abuse, which was to study the marijuana problem. The commission was chaired by former Pennsylvania governor Raymond P. Shafer. It released its report in March 1972 and basically called for decriminalizing possession and private use of marijuana. "Neither the marihuana user nor the drug itself can be said to constitute a danger to public safety. . . . Therefore, the Commission recommends . . . [the] possession of marijuana for personal use no longer be an offense, [and that the] casual distribution of small amounts of marihuana for no remuneration, or insignificant remuneration no longer be an offense."[31]

Both the Nixon administration and Congress were adamantly opposed to these recommendations, and neither branch made efforts to implement them. In a 2002 release of President Nixon's White House tapes, Nixon is heard saying, in response to the commission's findings, "You know, it's a funny thing, every one of those bastards that are out for legalizing marijuana is Jewish. What the Christ is the matter with the Jews, Bob? What is the matter with them? I suppose it is because most of them are psychiatrists.[32]

If the 1950s was a decade of stiffer federal penalties for drug use, the 1960s began a kinder, gentler approach: emphasizing drug treatment over incarceration and dropping convictions if people changed their behavior. The Narcotic Addict Rehabilitation Act of 1966 allowed treatment as an alternative to jail, the Alcoholic and Narcotic Addict Rehabilitation Amendments of 1968 provided block grants to the states to start addiction treatment centers, and the Drug Abuse Control Amendments of 1968 allowed drug sentences to be suspended and one's record to be wiped clean if there were no further violations within the year.

The 1970s and 1980s, on the other hand, saw Congress promote the growth of the substance abuse bureaucracy. It established the Alcohol, Drug Abuse, and Mental Health Administration (ADAMHA) in 1973 and the Drug Enforcement Administration (DEA) in 1973. The ADAMHA Reorganization Act in 1992 transferred the National Institute on Drug Abuse, the National Institute of Mental Health, and the National Institute on Alcohol Abuse and Alcoholism to the National Institutes of Health and incorporated ADAMHA's programs into a new agency called the Substance Abuse and Mental Health Services Administration.

Other federal legislation during this time further expanded substance abuse treatment efforts: the Drug Abuse Office and Treatment Act of 1972; the Methadone Control Act of 1973; the Drug Abuse Treatment and Control Amendments of 1974 and 1978; the Alcohol and Drug Abuse Education Amendments of 1978; the Drug Abuse Prevention, Treatment, and Rehabilitation Amendments of 1980; the Drug Offenders Act of 1984; the Analogue (Designer Drug) Act of 1986; and the Anti-Drug Abuse Act of 1988, which established the Office of National Drug Control Policy (the drug czar's office).

Despite this dizzying array of laws, agencies, treaties, and coordinated efforts, drug use continued to grow. It reached its peak in the late 1970s and trended downward until 1990, after which it has leveled (see figure 4.1).

RECENT ISSUES RELATED TO DRUG PROHIBITION

Medical Marijuana

The only successful push-back against drug prohibition has been efforts to legalize marijuana for medical use. Fifteen states and the District of

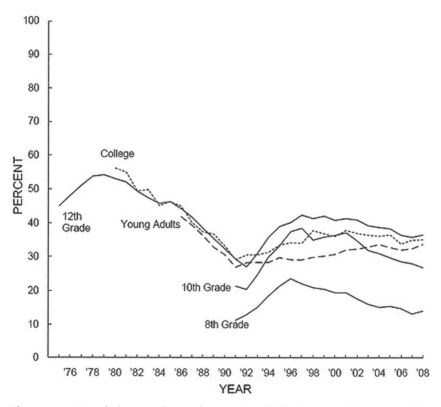

Figure 4.1. Trends in annual prevalence of an illicit drug use index across five populations. Source: *Monitoring the Future National Survey Results on Drug Use, 1975–2008,* vol. 2 (Ann Arbor: University of Michigan Press, 2009), 55.

Columbia now allow individuals with certain chronic diseases to legally purchase and possess limited amounts of marijuana if so recommended or prescribed by a physician. The specifics vary from state to state, but the qualifying diseases usually include cancer, glaucoma, AIDS, multiple sclerosis, chronic pain, or muscle spasms. California was the first state to pass a medical marijuana law in 1996, followed by Alaska (1998), Washington (1998), Oregon (1998), Maine (1999), Colorado (2000), Hawaii (2000), Nevada (2000), Montana (2004), Vermont (2004), Rhode Island (2006), New Mexico (2007), the District of Columbia (2010), Michigan (2008), New Jersey (2010), and Arizona (2010).

Legalizing marijuana for recreational purposes has not been as successful. California voters in 2010 turned down a referendum to legalize, tax, and regulate marijuana by 54 to 46 percent. On the other hand, Californians did decriminalize marijuana possession starting in 2011. If caught with less than one ounce, the infraction is treated like a parking ticket, with a fine of $100. As of late 2010, thirteen states and the city of Denver have decriminalized but not legalized the possession of small amounts of marijuana.

The obvious legal issue with medical marijuana laws is that they fly in the face of the federal Controlled Substance Act. After California passed their initiative in 1996, the nation's drug czar, retired Army General Barry McCaffrey, threatened to have the DEA pull the license of any physician who recommended or prescribed the drug. This move was defeated in a U.S. district court ruling in 2000.[33] The court ruled that the U.S. government could not punish physicians for voicing their professional opinions that were based on their best medical judgments.

To clarify matters, the U.S. Department of Justice in 2009 disseminated guidance to federal prosecutors that basically said that the United States would not prosecute "individuals whose actions are in clear and unambiguous compliance with existing state laws providing for the medical use of marijuana."[34]

Swelling Prison Populations

Illegal drug users are overrepresented among the criminal population and not just because of their drug use. In a 2008 study of people booked into jail—for any reason—in ten metropolitan areas, in which 85 percent agreed to voluntary urine testing, the number of positive urines for illicit drugs ranged from 49 percent in Washington, D.C., to 87 percent in Chicago.[35] The drug-using lifestyle correlates with and likely leads to other criminal behaviors.

In 2009, law enforcement officers nationwide made an estimated 13,687,241 arrests (excepting traffic violations). Of these, 1,663,582 were for drug violations, over half of which were for marijuana possession.[36]

According to Ethan Nadelmann of the Drug Policy Alliance Network, there were 50,000 people behind bars on nonviolent drug charges in 1980, and now there are half a million.[37] Currently, the United States has 5 percent of the world's population but close to 25 percent of the world's prisoners. According to the Bureau of Justice Statistics, as of June 30, 2009, state and federal correctional authorities had jurisdiction over 1,617,478 prisoners.[38] Another 767,620 inmates were housed in local and county jails.

Figure 4.2 shows the rapid growth in the prison population since the "war on drugs" began in earnest in the 1970s. While it is estimated that a quarter of the U.S. prison population is serving time for drug crimes, the growth of convictions for nondrug crimes is likely related to a general disregard for many laws that the drug-using lifestyle naturally entails.

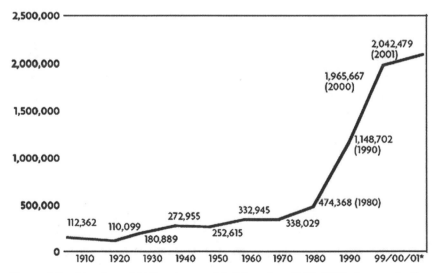

Figure 4.2. Number of U.S. prison and jail inmates, 1910–2000. Source: Justice Policy Institute, U.S. Department of Justice.

Drug Trade Violence and Police Corruption

One of the unintended consequences of the war on drugs is that prohibition creates a highly profitable black market. For many years, Mexican authorities tolerated their illicit drug trade, which was peaceful and made little noise. In 2006, President Felipe Calderón, at the urging of the United States, declared an all-out drug war, and by late 2011, there had been over 40,000 deaths as a consequence—with no apparent diminution in the amount of drugs that flow into the United States.

The drug-related violence in Mexico has been brutal. In October 2010, gunmen invaded a private drug treatment center in Tijuana and executed thirteen men at close range. Several days later, fifteen people were gunned down while working at a car wash. Most of these were clients of a drug rehab center in Tepic, Mexico. Rehab centers are common places for cartel members to "hide" when they wish to leave their former associates and change their lives.

In September 2010, a group of twenty employed family men were found buried in a mass grave near Acapulco. They were vacationing together and were mistakenly thought to be members of a rival gang.

The town of Ciudad Mier, in the state of Tamaulipas across the border from Texas, used to have a population of 6,000 and was a popular tourist destination. In early 2010, rival gangs turned it into a "slaughterhouse." One person was hanged live from a tree in the central plaza and dismembered in broad daylight. Detached heads were found outside the city limits. The town was subsequently abandoned by its residents because of cartel violence.[39]

Policing is largely ineffective. In reporting on the devastation in Tamaulipas, the *Wall Street Journal* noted that much of the brutality goes unreported and that citizens have to rely on social media to make sure that there are no outbreaks of violence on the routes normally taken to work or school.[40]

President Calderón announced in late 2010 that he wanted to abolish local police departments and use only federal agents to maintain security. The reason: almost all local law enforcement agencies have officers on the payrolls of the cartels. An investigative report in *Rolling Stone* magazine recently revealed how paid informants from competing cartels often inhabit the same local police stations. In Monterrey, for example, about half of the 750 local police officers have been fired on suspicion of links to organized crime. The magazine also detailed, however, that federal agents are not immune. In 2008, the feds raided a cartel party on the outskirts of Mexico City and seized the drugs, money, and prostitutes for their own wild party.[41] In an investigation of 400 federal police officers, 90 percent have been linked to the cartels.

In October 2010, over 100 tons of marijuana—with an estimated street value of $340 million—were seized in Baja California in one of the largest drug busts in Mexican history. The marijuana was hidden inside cargo containers stored in a warehouse in Tijuana, just across the border from San Diego.

The disconcerting issue about such discoveries is this: how can so much marijuana evade scrutiny all the way to the Mexico–U.S. border? Mexico has federal and military checkpoint operations over the course of all major roads and freeways. The answer, of course, is that the cartels control these checkpoints. With an estimated annual value of $20 billion, the Mexico-to-U.S. drug trade seems well positioned to absorb these occasional interdictions.

In the United States, drug-related violence appears to be closely connected to the growth of street gangs and syndicates. This has a long history, of course, dating to the 1920s. But gang-related violence dropped precipitously with the repeal of alcohol prohibition and did not reappear until the explosion of drug use in the 1960s and 1970s. This period saw the creation of the Cripps and Bloods in Los Angeles, whose primary source of financial support comes from drug trafficking. Following the crack cocaine epidemic in the 1980s, the DEA reported connections between these street gangs and drug sales in 46 states.[42] Numerous other gangs arose around the country, such as Chicago's Vice Lords. Turf battles between gangs have generated much of the violence that is characteristic of decaying urban settings.

In the late 1980s, a retired Detroit police officer summed up the state of affairs:

> It's like feudal China, there are pockets of entrenched drug operation all over the city. . . . You have warlords over little areas that control their little fiefdoms. There are young people acting as contractors for the warlords. . . . Kids and adults see the warlords spreading money and fame. They want some of that money. Soon as we put away one bunch, another one takes its place. Then you got professional people, like lawyers, giving these punks their service. Dope has made these characters think they're rich and powerful.[43]

A 2006 assessment produced by the U.S. Department of Justice showed how gangs have evolved from turf-oriented to profit-driven, criminal enterprises controlling wide swaths of wholesale distribution. Some national-level street gangs have as many as 100,000 members and associates.[44]

In general, the harder the government tries to stop the flow of banned substances, the more violent the market becomes. This was as true in the 1920s as it is today. Harvard economist and CATO fellow Jeffrey Miron[45] has examined the relationship last century between federal dollars spent enforcing prohibition and the prevailing homicide rate (see figures 4.3 and 4.4). It should be no surprise to learn that the homicide rate climbed significantly during alcohol prohibition and after President Nixon declared in 1971 that drug use was "public enemy number one."

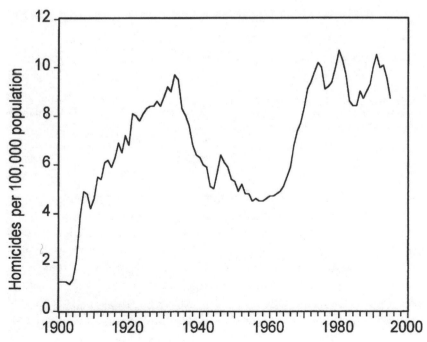

Figure 4.3. Homicides over time in the United States. Source: Jeffrey A. Miron, "Violence and the U.S. Prohibitions of Drugs and Alcohol," *American Law and Economics Review* 1–2 (1999): 78–114.

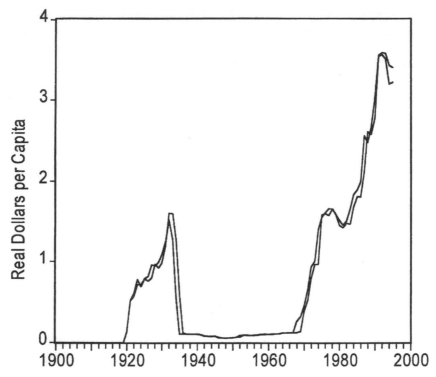

Figure 4.4. Federal expenditures on prohibition. Source: Jeffrey A. Miron, "Violence and the U.S. Prohibitions of Drugs and Alcohol," *American Law and Economics Review* 1–2 (1999): 78–114.

Designer Drugs

One of the limitations of drug prohibition is how "chemical entrepreneurs" are able to stay two steps ahead of the prohibition bureaucracy. While the Controlled Substance Act allows regulatory agencies, such as the DEA, to independently ban new substances whose properties are similar to drugs already prohibited, there is a lag between identification of the new drugs and the regulatory engines that will eventually prohibit them. Consequently, any entrepreneur with a background in synthetic chemistry can create new compounds that are slight variations on prohibited substances but that are perfectly legal for a time. Such drugs enjoy huge popularity in nightclubs and are briskly sold online. Such drugs are marketed with the caveat "not for human consumption," helping them stay within the law.

Recent examples of "legal highs" are K2 (similar to marijuana), Meow Meow (similar to amphetamine), and Nopaine (similar to Ritalin). As soon as the regulatory bureaucracy catches up to these drugs, the chemists have moved on to related compounds that are not yet illegal. As with similar but banned substances, these drugs can be dangerous, and overdoses have led to deaths. These drugs do not undergo safety testing at the level of the Food and Drug Administration. According to the *Wall Street Journal*, one such chemical entrepreneur conducts his own "safety" tests as follows: "We'll all sit with a pen and a pad, some good music on, and one person who's straight who's watching everything."[46]

Black Market Sophistication

Given the profitable nature of the drug trade, traffickers have become quite creative as they move drugs in and around the black market. There exist, for instance, numerous tunnels between Tijuana, Mexico, and San Diego, California. From 2007 to 2010, authorities discovered seventy-five of them. In November 2010, two tunnels were discovered that stored thirty-two and twenty tons of marijuana, respectively. One tunnel started in the floor of a kitchen in Tijuana, dropped down ninety feet, and traveled over half a mile before it exited inside two different warehouses in San Diego. It was equipped with rail tracks, carts, electricity, and ventilation. The tunnel was reinforced with wood and cinder blocks.[47] No one knows how many tunnels connect the two countries, but in all likelihood, authorities have only scratched the surface.

Other schemes to transport drugs have included getting couriers to fake medical emergencies if they are caught crossing the border, then refusing care at hospitals and running away. Some travel in ultralight aircraft that literally fly under the radar as they cross the border. Others paint vehicles to resemble U.S. Border Control vehicles or DHL delivery trucks. Others have smuggled drugs in golf balls, diapers, and even insects. Peruvian police once seized 1,540 pounds of pepper-coated cocaine bricks hidden inside a giant frozen squid that was headed for the United States.

One of my patients in prison told me a trick he learned to help fund his methamphetamine habit. He would set up sham checking accounts and then write bad checks for cash. When he was well into a cycle of meth, banks would start to refuse him because of his emaciated appearance. They correctly suspected that he was a drug addict. He soon learned to tell bankers up front that his poor physical appearance was from undergoing chemotherapy for cancer. He was never turned down again.

INTERNATIONAL DRUG CONTROL EFFORTS

The year 2011 was the fiftieth anniversary of the UN Single Convention on Narcotic Drugs. While the United Nations says that the provisions in the convention "remain sound and relevant," it also reports that the value of the illicit drug trade in some parts of the world now exceeds that of the legitimate economy.[48]

The UN Office on Drugs and Crime monitors worldwide drug control efforts. It estimates that between 149 million and 272 million people worldwide used illicit drugs in 2009. Over the last decade, drug control efforts have led to a doubling of the amount of seized drugs,[49] but increased cultivation and consumption rates have kept the United Nations from being able to prevent and control drug trafficking.

The major global trends in the last decade have been that cocaine use has increased in Europe and South America while it has decreased in North America. Opium production has increased 80 percent in the last decade, and now heroin use is spreading to Africa. The other major trends have been the increased use of designer drugs and prescription drug abuse.

The world opiate/heroin markets have been estimated to be worth $68 billion annually. In most years, over 90 percent of the world's opium crop comes from Afghanistan. In 2009, several diseases attacked poppy fields, and Afghanistan's share dropped to 63 percent. When the Taliban was in power, it had suppressed production to about one-fourth to one-third what it is today.[50] In exile, the Taliban has been supporting opium production, which in turn supports it with about $155 million annually. The Taliban collects a 10 percent "tax" from farmers in return for protection from eradication efforts under the direction of joint Allied–Afghan government forces.

The difficulty with eradication efforts is the fact that opium is so lucrative for poor farmers. A *New Yorker* article[51] in 2007 profiled just what is at stake: farmers get about $33 per acre for growing wheat and $500 to $700 for growing poppies. Eradication teams are frequently attacked by farmers and Taliban soldiers, who rely on leaks from inside the Afghan government about which fields are slated for destruction. During a monthlong 2007 operation in the Helmand province, only about 4 percent of the crop was eradicated. Observers noted that fields belonging to members of President Karzai's tribe—the Populazi—seemed to be untouched. In 2010, General Stanley McChrystal announced that U.S. forces would no longer take part in eradication efforts.[52]

Fifty countries and international organizations have signed on to the 2003 UN-sponsored "Paris Pact," which is devoted to stopping opium cultivation and trafficking out of Afghanistan. Since 2003, opium production in Afghanistan had more than doubled[53] before its disease-induced decline in 2009. Worldwide, about 16 to 20 percent of opium gets seized,[54] but since Afghanistan can produce twice as much opium as is currently consumed, the overall significance of these seizures is debatable.

The world's cocaine market has been estimated to be $85 billion annually, which is about half what it was in 1995. The drop in value is due to slightly decreased consumption and greatly decreased prices. The United States is still the largest cocaine market, consuming about 36 percent of the world's supply, but over the last decade, cocaine consumption in Europe has doubled.[55]

Almost all the world's cocaine comes from coca plants grown in Peru, Bolivia, and Colombia. In the early 1980s, most of that crop was flown to markets in North America and Europe. When the United States began shooting down transport planes, the traffickers moved to ground and sea modes of delivery. A Government Accountability Office report in 1984 stated that these interdiction efforts left cocaine trafficking "virtually uninterrupted."[56]

The Medellin and Cali drug cartels had virtual control of cocaine markets by the 1990s. These organizations dissolved after the deaths and arrests of their leaders. Traffickers quickly adjusted by forming numerous independent, small alliances, and the cocaine markets did not miss a beat.[57]

In 2009, President Ayma of Bolivia pleaded with the United Nations to reverse the Single Convention's prohibition of the consumption of coca leaves. In a letter to the editor in the *New York Times*,[58] he noted that his countrymen have a long tradition—going back to at least 3000 BC—of chewing the plant. He claimed that it helps eliminate the sensation of hunger, provides energy for long workdays, and helps battle altitude sickness. According to the convention, Bolivians who do this are criminals who violate international law. Ayma called it an unacceptable and absurd state of affairs.

The marijuana (cannabis) herb is grown all over the world, and it generally supplies local markets. Cannabis resin, on the other hand, is a concentrated form that is shipped to distant markets. The largest producers of resin are Afghanistan, Morocco, Lebanon, and Nepal/India. Cannabis is the most commonly consumed illicit drug with between 125 million and 203 million people consuming it within the last year.[59]

Amphetamine-type stimulants (amphetamine, methamphetamine, methcathinone, and ecstasy) are synthetic substances that are not geographically limited; they are produced in laboratories wherever there is a market for them. Methamphetamine is by far the most widely used drug of this group, and control of methamphetamine is through control of the meth labs where it is produced. In 2009, there were 10,600 seizures of these labs reported to the United Nations, almost all of which were in the United States. By contrast, Mexico, which produces large amounts of methamphetamines, seized 191 laboratories in 2009, up from twenty-one in 2008. On the other hand, Mexico seized more cannabis in 2009 than did the United States.[60]

Because of the difficulty with interdiction efforts, many countries have been trying innovative approaches on the demand side—on the users themselves. Switzerland is one example.

In the late 1980s and early 1990s, Swiss officials sanctioned Zurich's infamous Platzspitz park for open drug use; it became known as "needle park." The thinking was that if addicts could use drugs unmolested by police and health officials could monitor and promote safe drug use, then much of the disease and sordidness of the drug culture would dissipate. What happened instead is that addicts and drug suppliers came from all over Europe, and up to 1,000 addicts came to the park each day, and there were many acts of indecency. In February 1992, police shut down the park after numerous complaints from local residents and expanding rates of diseases.[61]

Swiss officials then tried a different "harm reduction" approach: free heroin maintenance in all major cities and towns along with regular health care for addicts. After the first ten years of the program, HIV rates decreased, crime decreased, and the overall health and social functioning of heroin addicts improved.[62] The Swiss were impressed enough with this approach that 68 percent of respondents in a 2008 national referendum voted to continue the program.[63]

Policing and interdiction efforts are frequently compromised by the corruption of public officials and the sophistication of black markets. Stopping drug trafficking is like playing the Whac-A-Mole game—suppress it in one location, and it quickly appears elsewhere. Traffickers have so much cash that, when they are not paying off public officials, they are having to find creative ways to launder their wealth. Currently, reinvesting money in legitimate businesses has proved to be successful.[64]

CONCLUSION

Drug prohibition laws arose out of antipathy toward immigrants and minorities and out of corporate self-interest, but they now provide important support for the disease model of substance abuse. According to the DEA, illegal drugs are illegal because they are harmful.[65] Reasonable people have difficulty stepping back and fairly assessing the damage these laws create because they believe that they are preventing the spread of addictive diseases.

The next several chapters dissect the disease model of substance abuse. I argue that the available evidence does not support the model. Instead, the evidence supports a much narrower finding: it shows why quitting can be hard. The "out-of-control" drug addict is not the victim of a disease; rather, he or she is an opportunist living off the social policies that follow from the disease model.

5

THE POWER OF
PARADIGMS

When President Obama announced in his 2009 inaugural address that "we will restore science to its rightful place," he was talking about not placing limits on science but rather expanding its influence. This was understood to be a counterpolicy to the Bush administration's practice of not always following the recommendations of the scientific community. Bush was said to have "politicized" science. With the new administration, science would be set free and restored to its rightful place of arbitrating what is true of the natural world.

Waxing nostalgic about scientific truth telling, however, will cause one to miss one of the bigger stories in science over the last fifty years, namely, that scientific work is not as objective as traditionally thought.

One example of flawed objectivity is the widely recognized "observer effect." This happens when scientists inadvertently alter the natural world simply through their attempts to observe it. For instance, sticking a cool glass thermometer in a hot fluid-filled jar causes some energy to be absorbed by the glass thermometer before it records the now-lowered temperature of the fluid. In particle physics, finding the location of an electron requires that it first interact with a photon, thereby altering its location before it is even seen. Another example occurs when researchers administer questionnaires. This often produces skewed opinions because respondents typically exert some effort to please their surveyors.

Even when the natural world can be accurately observed, scientists often let a priori assumptions influence what they see. This is where science philosopher Thomas Kuhn made his mark. In his book, *The Structure of Scientific Revolutions* (1962),[1] Kuhn argued that scientific observation is heavily influenced by scientists' own expectations. These expectations, he argued, are driven by paradigms or models. A paradigm is an organizing construct that gives meaning to the facts that scientific work uncovers. Paradigms are important because facts—when they are discovered—are not always well understood and often appear to contradict each other. Paradigms provide a larger story—a superstory—that more or less makes everything fit together in a coherent fashion.

Paradigms serve the natural human desire to have the world make sense. Scientists are no different than others in this regard. Paradigms also provide social cohesion for the many disparate and isolated researchers who work on obscure scientific problems. No matter how small or esoteric a scientist's own research, a governing paradigm allows his or her efforts to fit a larger and more significant story that can then be shared and appreciated by others in the field.

Paradigms do not have to be accurate to be useful, and history has provided many examples. Consider the state of astronomy faced by Copernicus (1473–1543) and Galileo (1564–1642). At that time, astronomers believed that the center of the universe was the earth, around which the sun and planets orbited. This paradigm, known as geocentrism, was first formulated by the Greek astronomer Claudius Ptolemy (AD 90–168). This model fit solidly within the theological and political traditions of the Roman Catholic Church, which was then the ruling power of much of the Western world. Since God had made earth to be the center of the universe—a claim that the Church has made throughout its existence—geocentrism was important to the Church's ongoing prestige and authority.

As new observations of planetary movements became known—observations that should have nullified geocentricism—scientists were able to make the new data fit the geocentric paradigm. For instance, it was noted that in the night sky, planets sometimes traveled in one direction for part of the year and then appeared to travel in the opposite direction at other times. Astronomers in the third and fourth centuries modified the paradigm to account for these observations by creating what are called "epicycles."

In figure 5.1, the earth is just off center (B). A planet is traveling in a small epicycle (A) as its main trajectory (C) circles the earth. Both the epicycle and its main trajectory travel in a counterclockwise direc-

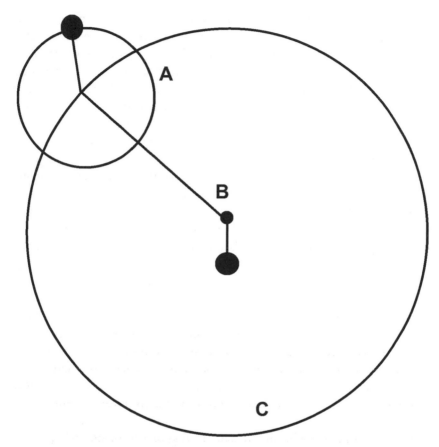

Figure 5.1. Depiction of a geocentric epicycle.

tion. From the viewpoint of the earth, the planet could then be seen traveling one direction part of the year and the opposite direction at another time. As astronomers' observations of the planets became more refined, they were forced to create even more epicycles. The Ptolemaic paradigm, with its "epicycles upon epicycles," became strained but still, at the time of Copernicus, gave a coherent and largely satisfactory account of the movement of the planets.

Copernicus was the first to systematically challenge the geocentric model. His observations led him to believe that the earth and other planets circled the sun, a model called heliocentrism. His famous book *De revolutionibus orbium coelestium*, published the year of his death, was not accepted at the time but would later be seen to have played a crucial role in ushering in the scientific revolution.

Sixty years later, the Italian scientist Galileo took up the cause of heliocentrism. He had refined the telescope and was able to improve on Copernicus's observations. Galileo witnessed, for example, all four phases of Venus. The geocentric model predicted that only two phases would be seen, whereas the heliocentric model predicted that all four would be seen. Copernicus and Galileo helped form the modern view of the solar system, but geocentrism's demise was not complete until the nineteenth century, when telescopes underwent further refinement and astronomers were even less wed to Ptolemy's views.

The Copernican revolution illustrates several important points about paradigms. The first is that paradigms can actually make sense of the natural world even when they are wildly off the mark. This happens because paradigms are constructs. They are not part of the facts; they are designed to fit the facts. If the fit is good, scientists often will use the paradigm to explain the facts. This intellectual sleight of hand helps scientists feel confident about their work and gives laymen the impression that scientists know more than they actually do.

Second, paradigms have intrinsic tendencies that resist change. According to Kuhn, most scientific work is concerned with reinforcing prevailing paradigms, not with challenging them. And when paradigms acquire political clout, their resistance to change is even greater. Galileo pushed his views into the highest reaches of the Catholic Church. Father Robert Bellarmine, the Vatican's chief theologian and point man for dealing with Galileo, wrote the scientist in 1613 to explain that heliocentrism was dangerous because it irritated all the philosophers and theologians and also because it violated the faith and the holy scriptures.[2] Galileo's writings were eventually banned, and he was given a prison sentence that was commuted to house arrest for the remainder of his life.

When paradigms do change, it is only after long ideological or political struggles. And then they do not evolve as much as get replaced. Younger scientists not steeped in the traditions of an established paradigm develop new ways of thinking that lead to years of debates with their elders. Followers of the old paradigm often do not adopt the new way of thinking. Rather, the new paradigm prevails when members of the old school die off.

There are other examples of the influence of paradigms. In the 1770s, when Lavoisier was studying gases, he could not "see" oxygen—

a gas he was experimentally producing—because he was wed to the phlogiston paradigm of air. It was only after he discarded phlogiston that he recognized oxygen. His contemporary Joseph Priestly held on to the phlogiston theory to the end of his life and thus never recognized oxygen's presence even though he was producing it in the same manner as Lavoisier.[3]

A more recent example was D. L. Rosenhan's famous study in which eight normal study subjects gained admission to twelve psychiatric hospitals merely by reporting to doctors that they had heard a voice saying "empty," "hollow," or "thud." Immediately on admission, they were to report, if asked, that the symptom was no longer present. They were instructed not to behave strangely in any other way. After an average stay of nineteen days, each patient was diagnosed with schizophrenia.[4] The psychiatrists "saw" mental illness even when it did not exist. They acted like the proverbial man with a hammer who sees nothing but nails.

Paradigms survive when they appear to explain the workings of the natural world. They also survive when they supply important narratives for their stakeholders. Before dissecting the neuroscience behind the disease model, it will be important to review how the model serves its main stakeholders: doctors, politicians, and addicts.

THE DOCTOR'S NARRATIVE

The modern disease model arose in the mid-twentieth century at a time when the scientific community needed a boost to its reputation. Science was blamed for a technological revolution that had created crowded urban settings and had put many people out of work. It was also science that ushered in the nuclear age. The vast devastation from the atomic bomb brought a new era of angst to post–World War II America. Medical science was also a target of criticism because doctors generally had liberal prescribing practices and were held responsible for getting so many people addicted to drugs and alcohol. From 1920 to 1933, for instance, the only way to legally purchase alcohol was with a doctor's prescription.

As shown in chapter 3, the medical profession did not create the modern disease model; the profession merely appropriated it. The model brought new prestige to the profession, as it now appeared that medical science could explain and treat deviant human behavior. Prior to this, claims about deviancy were the purview of religion, philosophy, or personal opinion.

The medical community was the biggest beneficiary, of course, when the federal government sent block grants, formula grants, and project grants to the states to establish treatment clinics. In the private sector, states began to require that health insurance companies cover substance abuse treatment. And with the establishment of the National Institute on Alcohol Abuse and Alcoholism and the National Institute on Drug Abuse (NIDA), the disease model became a permanent fixture on the political landscape. Today, addiction treatment is a $25 billion annual industry, but, as I show in chapter 7, rehab is a gateway to the much more lucrative mental health industry, which is expected to be worth $203 billion in 2014.[5]

Understandably, the medical profession protects its turf. The first line of defense is the obfuscation that laypeople face when they encounter medical jargon. Visit the NIDA website, for example, and one of the first links is to the booklet *Drugs, Brain and Behavior—The Science of Addictions*. Laypeople are immediately exposed to a brain scan and are led to discussions of neurotransmitters, positron-emission tomography, dendrites, axons, genetics, and neuronal synapses.

As a thought experiment, consider what buying deck chairs would be like if product literature and salespeople stressed the scientific underpinnings of wood; how the polysaccharide cellulose is made up of glucose monomers; how, because of the orientation of the glycosidic bonds linking the glucose residues, the polymer is able to form rigid fibrils; and how this rigidity is further reinforced by the absence of side chains and the presence of hydroxyl groups and oxygen atoms, thereby allowing a sturdy linear orientation for wood fibers. Buyers might think that they are unqualified to buy deck chairs and might instead feel the need to hire a materials engineer.

But get past the medical verbiage, and if you are confident enough to criticize the disease model, you will be the target of the profession's most vicious attack: charges of stigmatization.

The word "stigma" derives from the Latin word for tattoo or a brand placed on a criminal. It can be traced back to the Greek (to stick or prick). Historically, a "stigma" was a physical mark for slaves, traitors, and criminals.

In a recent editorial in a medical journal, a leading addiction researcher, responding to attempts by state legislators to limit spending on addiction treatment, said, "In the coming century, physicians' task is to confront these recurring attitudes of moralism and stigma."[6]

According to the Dr. Nora Volkow, the director of the NIDA,

Stigma is an enormous obstacle to more effective drug abuse treatment . . . [it] lead[s] to self-fulfilling predictions that those who are addicted cannot recover or ever play positive and productive social roles. . . . Today, researchers and informed, creative clinicians are achieving the understanding and management skills that eventually will erase the stigma surrounding drug addiction.[7]

Stigma is said to keep people from seeking treatment,[8] to encourage substance abusers to adopt deviant identities, to lead to lower wages at work and trouble finding housing, and to also cause low self confidence.[9] Whether any of these outcomes might be due to actual substance abuse rather than to stigma is never given much consideration.

Accusations of stigma do more than keep critics at bay. They also frame an artificial debate. You either see addicts as ill and in need of treatment or stigmatize them and want them punished. There are no other options.

One issue that is never raised, however, is how labeling addicts with a genetic brain disease might impart a stigma of its own, resulting in unintended consequences. A group of sociologists noted in the 1960s that the sick role can legitimize deviant drinking patterns and "may serve to 'lock' the deviant drinker into a nexus of role expectations as well as changing his self-concept."[10] If this is true, then who is stigmatizing whom?

It is ironic that proponents of the disease model are always the first to heap charges of stigmatization on their critics. This is an attempt to shame them. This only proves that advocates of the disease model agree that shame is a good thing; they just want to be able to control to whom it should apply.

In the end, widespread claims of stigma are paper tigers. They are designed to protect the disease model from scrutiny. An Institute of Medicine publication appears to have captured what is at stake: "When policymakers view drug abusers as untreatable or undeserving of public support, treatment programs, insurance coverage, and research and training programs may be underfunded or abolished."[11]

CHAPTER 5

THE POLITICIAN'S NARRATIVE

The disease model fits squarely within the twentieth century's progressive political tradition, wherein science is believed to be the only legitimate means for solving human problems. By supporting the disease model, politicians simultaneously stake two popular claims: they care about people, and they believe in the authority of science. This goes a long way on the campaign trail.

A key tenet of the disease model is that addicts have lost control of their behavior. This greatly expands the politician's role. If addicts cannot control themselves, there is no logical limit to the amount of help they require. No area of an addict's life is beyond the reach of compassion-minded politicians. This explains the expanding amount of social services (see chapter 7) that federal, state, and local governments are providing for our nation's substance abusers.

The growth of progressive politics was made possible in part by the theory of biological reductionism. This is a widely shared paradigm within the scientific community. It views human behavior as being controlled by genes and brain biochemistry. Politicians are attracted to biological reductionism because it places them (along with scientists) on a higher ontological plane than the masses. Policymakers begin to see themselves as thoughtful, reflective people who are able to break away from the limits of their own biochemistry to devise intelligent legislation that addresses the problems caused by other people's biochemistries.

Drug prohibition laws reinforce this special status. Even though such laws cause great harm to society, repealing them would be an implicit recognition that the masses would have to be trusted with habit-forming substances. Prohibition laws maintain the parent–child relationship between the enlightened rulers and the biologically driven masses.

The paradox of allowing some habit-forming drugs to be legal, such as alcohol and nicotine, is partly explained by the fact that politicians themselves like to self-indulge but also because legal drugs can be used to serve political agendas. An example is the $206 billion deal struck in 1998 between forty-six state attorneys general and the four major tobacco companies, which had 99 percent of the market at that time. The tobacco companies agreed to make annual payments to the states over twenty-five years, and the states agreed to protect the companies against competition from smaller tobacco companies and to give them immunity from further liability. South Carolina's attorney general has remarked that states have become obligated to "prop up big tobacco to make sure they sell enough cigarettes to make payments to the states."[12]

Whether drugs are legal or illegal is less important than whether they are viewed as major threats to society. With that claim, policymakers expand their roles as guardians of the masses.

THE ADDICT'S NARRATIVE

To say that the disease model can function as an excuse for addictive behavior is to point out the obvious. Fortunately, federal and state statutes, as well as legal precedent, do not typically allow the disease model to mitigate or excuse criminal conduct. Statements like "My genes made me do it" or "I couldn't resist the craving" may quell an angry spouse, but we can all be thankful that they do not often move judges and juries.

The real narrative power of the disease model, however, is more subtle and is consistent with our culture's Judeo-Christian tradition: the disease model provides a mechanism for redemption. It is what those prominent, early members of Alcoholics Anonymous (AA) sought. To appropriate the redemption, one must 1) admit to having a disease and 2) be willing to enter treatment. The moral absolution is instantaneous and can be appropriated as often as needed. No matter how many times one relapses, admitting the existence of a problem and expressing a desire to go to treatment recaptures one's moral standing. Multiple relapses—and multiple admissions—prove, to those willing to believe, the tragic nature of the disease and the never-ending human struggle to overcome it.

The evolution of rehab as redemption started at the dawn of the temperance movement with the rise of the "drunkard narrative." This was modeled after Christian salvation stories of the time. Historian Elaine Parsons has examined the nineteenth-century temperance literature and has identified several common themes of drunkard narratives: the eventual drunkard at first shows great promise in life, then he faces harsh external circumstances, he chooses the wrong kind of friends, he loses control of his life when he starts to drink, and then he is redeemed through strong outside forces.[13]

These tales of debauchery were largely fueled by the Washingtonian movement, which attracted over 600,000 drunkards from 1840 to 1845.[14] According to William L. White, a chronicler of the history of addiction treatment,

> The Washingtonian meetings were high drama. Instead of the debates, formal speeches, and abstract principles that had been on the standard temperance meeting agenda, the main bill of fare at a Washingtonian meeting was experience sharing—confessions of alcoholic debauchery followed by glorious accounts of personal reformation. . . . This ritual of public confession and public signing of the pledge carried great emotional power for those participating.[15]

Following a Washingtonian meeting in Boston, one news report claimed, "We believe more tears were never shed by an audience in one evening than flowed last night. . . . Old gray haired men sobbed like children, and the noble and honorable bowed their heads and wept."[16]

While the Washingtonian movement died as quickly as it arose, its format was resurrected by AA in 1935. Anyone who has attended an AA meeting knows that experience sharing is a big part.

Sociologist Robin Room has noted that "for the storyteller, addiction is an extremely serviceable plot motivator. The most outlandish and outrageous situation, episode or action can be made believable by portraying one of the characters as an addict. In stories, as in life, the addiction concept offers an apparent explanation of the otherwise inexplicable."[17]

The disease model's redemptive capacity is probably best illustrated by the way celebrities check into rehab whenever they are caught red-handed. Mel Gibson entered rehab after he hurled anti-Semitic insults at a female police officer during a drunk-driving arrest. Representative Patrick Kennedy (D-RI) sought help at the Mayo Clinic for his drug addiction shortly after he crashed his car into a barricade on Capitol Hill. When Congressman Mark Foley (R-FL) was nabbed exchanging sexually oriented emails with teenage boys, he said, "I strongly believe that I am an alcoholic and have accepted the need for immediate treatment for alcoholism and other behavioral problems." As one consultant from a crisis management firm said, checking into rehab lets you go from "villain to victim."[18]

In the end, accepting the disease model and going to rehab is the cultural equivalent of confessing one's sins and receiving forgiveness. The disease model provides immediate atonement. Interestingly, absolution comes not from staying sober but from going to rehab.

6

THE BRAIN ON DRUGS

B rain science has inherent limitations when it is invoked to explain human behavior. The problem is that scientists cannot see the mind; they can see only the brain. Looking through a microscope, scientists can see billions of neurons and the many blood vessels that nourish them, but scientists cannot see consciousness, awareness, or any other aspect of the mind. They cannot see thoughts, memories, fantasies, or guilt. In fact, there is nothing gained by observing brain cells that leads one to conclude that the mind even exists. We know it exists, though, because we individually experience it. I have consciousness, feelings, and thoughts; I can only assume that others do too.

This mind–brain conflict used to be a topic of debate until brain scientists flooded the conversation and pushed nonscientific perspectives to the side. Now the brain is used to explain everything. Nobel Prize neuroscientist Eric Kandel has said that "all behavior is the result of brain function. What we commonly call the mind is a set of operations carried out by the brain."[1]

Kandel is speaking paradigmatically, even if he does not come out and say it. No one knows how the brain carries out the mind or how it mediates behavior.[2] One has to rely on a paradigm to make these claims. Like Benjamin Rush, biological reductionists frequently make facile cause-and-effect connections between the brain and behavior. For any given behavior, they simply claim that it is caused by the brain. They cannot point to anatomical or physiological causes; they simply assert that the causes exist. They do this because their paradigm allows it.

The French philosopher René Descartes (1596–1650) might have been wrong when he said that the mind and brain are completely independent, but I think he was on to something when he implied that they are not the same thing. Whatever we think we know about the brain and behavior, there are volumes that we do not know, and it seems unlikely that empirical science has the tools to provide the answers.

What we do know is that the mind is incredibly resourceful and is not bound to obey brain-mediated biological urges. Consider, for instance, the act of fasting. The human appetite for food is arguably the most genetically compelling drive of all. Yet people routinely fast because they want to lose weight, fulfill religious obligations, or make political statements. Whatever the reason, fasting is successfully done only through the exertion of raw mental willpower. That food can be resisted at all is a testament to the mind's resourcefulness.

NEUROSCIENCE AND THE DISEASE MODEL

Dr. Nora Volkow, head of the National Institute on Drug Abuse (NIDA), has said that "through scientific inquiry, NIDA research has demonstrated that drug addiction is essentially a brain disease."[3]

As the rest of this chapter will demonstrate, Volkow's embrace of the disease model is done not by examining the science but by adopting a paradigm. Examining the science leads to much narrower conclusions that do not in any way support the disease paradigm.

We will examine the following three claims frequently made to support the disease model:

1. Addicts have diseased brains.
2. Addicts are genetically tainted individuals who have an inbred susceptibility to substance abuse.
3. Addictions are similar to other medical conditions, such as hypertension, cancer, and diabetes. All are marked by frequent relapses and the need for ongoing treatment.

ADDICTION AS BRAIN DISEASE

Volkow's predecessor at the NIDA, Dr. Alan Leshner, told a congressional committee in 1998 that "drug addiction is in fact an illness caused by the effects of prolonged drug use on the brain."[4] The popular HBO series *Addiction* repeatedly makes the brain disease claim. Consumer websites do the same.

True enough, it has been shown that chronic drug use leads to structural and physiological changes in the brain. These changes can be detected with imaging studies such as magnetic resonance imaging (MRI), functional MRI, positron-emission tomography (PET), and single-photon emission computed tomography (SPECT) scans.[5] Drug use, for instance, can lead to smaller frontal and prefrontal lobes, both important areas for mediating judgment and decision making. Other studies have shown that the sensation of craving is a drug-induced hypermetabolic state within part of the brain's reward center. PET and SPECT scans have shown how drugs of abuse flood the brain's reward center, leading to intense highs.

Other changes in the brain include the development of withdrawal symptoms. These are states of physiological and emotional arousal (sweating, tremors, nausea, anxiety, depression, or restlessness) that occur when one abruptly stops taking habit-forming drugs after a period of chronic use. Withdrawal symptoms are brain cell–mediated phenomena. Cells adapt electrochemically to the foreign chemicals in which they bathe. When that milieu changes—when someone abruptly stops consuming drugs or alcohol—the cells must readapt to the new drug-free environment. This unleashes the body's autonomic nervous system, translating into a temporary state of uncomfortable withdrawal symptoms.

The effects of chronic drug use, then, are intense highs, impaired judgment, poor impulse control, irritability, craving, and withdrawal. Craving and withdrawal can be immediately allayed by reconsuming one's drug of choice. This up-and-down experience is what is termed the "addictive cycle."

All drugs of abuse—nicotine, alcohol, amphetamines, marijuana, cocaine, and heroin—exert effects in the brain's pleasure center, called the mesolimbic dopamine reward system (MDRS). This group of cells lies deep within the brain. It is responsible for mediating the intense highs and lows of substance abuse. It is also responsible for natural feelings of euphoria. Gambling, sex, and other natural highs stimulate the same region.

The key anatomic components of the MDRS are the ventral tegmental area (VTA), nucleus accumbens, amygdala, hippocampus, and frontal lobes. The VTA neurons are dopamine rich and appear to be essential for the euphoric highs that come from substance abuse. Animals that have their VTAs destroyed show little interest in consuming addictive drugs.[6] The amygdala helps determine if the experience is pleasurable and, if so, records it in the hippocampus, the memory center of the brain. Projections to the frontal lobes help coordinate further stimulation if that is desired.

Chronic stimulation of the MDRS also prompts cellular changes that result in tolerance, where more of the drug is needed to produce the same level of euphoria. All these changes—tolerance, withdrawal, and craving—appear to be mediated or enhanced by neuroplasticity, which is the growth and expansion of nerve cells in the MDRS. Neuroplasticity leads to more connections between the cells within the MDRS and thus increased signaling. Over time, the MDRS lets drug users know when it wants to be fed—and increasingly so.

While these brain changes may seem compelling, they have to be viewed in a larger perspective. Consider the following four issues. The first is that these changes are reversible with abstinence. It may take several days or weeks, but the brain eventually returns to its preabused state. Cue-induced craving can take months to be reversed, as former smokers and brain scans will confirm, but the bulk of pressure from the addictive cycle is broken in a relatively short period of time.

Second, breaking the addictive cycle is not nearly as dramatic as Hollywood movies would have one believe. The image of the writhing, besotted addict being held down by burly hospital attendants in white garb is a cinematic creation. Most addicts I have ushered through the withdrawal process—even without attenuating medications—are much more likely to manifest withdrawal by arguing over the channel changer in the psychiatric dayroom. British writer and psychiatrist Theodore Dalrymple has written that heroin addicts often "admit with a laugh that anyone who says cold turkey is terrible is lying and more than likely trying to bluff his way to getting methadone."[7]

Third, disease model advocates like to point to research showing that laboratory mice will consume drugs to the point of exhaustion and even death.[8] This is apparently meant to support the argument that since drug-induced brain changes are enough to compel unstoppable drug use in some mammals, they are capable of doing so in all mammals. But this argument is pure sophistry. The fact that humans have powerful and complex minds is precisely what sets us apart from mice and what makes facile comparisons meaningless.

Finally, there is no physiologic difference between those who quit and those who do not. I have seen many severe addicts successfully quit cold turkey. Those who quit have to endure the same craving and withdrawal symptoms that others claim are the reasons they cannot quit. The only observable difference between the two groups appears to be, alas, more motivation in those who quit.

Whether drug-induced changes in the brain imply that substance abuse is a disease depends, of course, on how one defines a disease. But it is probably more accurate to view these changes as temporary states of neuroplasticity that are induced—and reversed—by nothing other than a person's behavior. Craving, withdrawal, and tolerance reflect the brain's normal reaction to the demands that are placed on it. Flood the brain with drugs or alcohol, and predictable changes take place. Stop using drugs and alcohol, and those changes are predictably reversed.

The Genetics Claim

One of the most important tenets of the disease model is that substance abuse is a genetic disorder. According to Dr. Enoch Gordis, former director of the National Institute on Alcohol Abuse and Alcoholism,

> Perhaps the single greatest influence on the scope and direction of alcohol research has been the finding that a portion of the vulnerability to alcoholism is genetic. This finding, more than any other, helped to establish the biological basis of alcoholism. . . . Today we know that approximately 50 to 60 percent of the risk for developing alcoholism is genetic.[9]

At first glance, the research on genetics appears compelling. Substance abuse tends to cluster in families, and this has been noticed for centuries. It does not exclusively run in families, as most cases have no family pattern. Most of the clustering, however, is accounted for by environment. It is modeled behavior. If one's parents, grandparents, aunts, and uncles go through life drinking and drugging—in good times and in bad—then these customs get passed to progeny as learned behavior and have nothing to do with genes.

Researchers, however, have been able to separate genetic from learned influences. They do this through twin and adoption studies. In twin studies, researchers examine concordance rates between identical and nonidentical twins. A concordance rate is the frequency that both twins have a disorder if one of them has it. If substance abuse has a genetic component, then identical twins, who share 100 percent of their genes, would be expected to have higher concordance rates than fraternal twins, who share 50 percent of their genes. A Swedish study[10] found a 54 percent concordance rate among identical twins for alcohol abuse and a 28 percent concordance rate among fraternal twins. Other studies have not found this relationship,[11] and some have found higher concordance rates among male but not female twins.

Adoption studies are another way to isolate genetic effects. Researchers follow children from substance-abusing biological parents who are adopted out at birth and are raised by non–substance-abusing parents. These results are compared with control groups of children from non–substance-abusing parents who are adopted out at birth. If substance abuse has a genetic component, you would expect children of substance-abusing biological parents—but raised in sober households—to have higher rates of substance abuse than control children whose biological parents were not substance abusers. Sure enough, a Danish study found that children from alcoholic parents had twice the number of alcohol problems and four times the diagnosis of alcoholism than did children from nonalcoholic parents.[12]

Let us now put this research into a broader context because there are several key issues that deserve attention. The first is that no single gene has been discovered that causes substance abuse. There have been claims that such genes exist, but none have survived close scrutiny. In 1990, for instance, Dr. Ernest P. Noble of the University of California, Los Angeles, and Dr. Kenneth Blum of the University of Texas, San Antonio, claimed to have discovered a gene coding for a type of dopamine receptor that they believed was a genetic marker for alcoholism. The finding was released to great fanfare—front-page coverage in the *New York Times* and a cover story in *Time* magazine. Subsequent attempts to replicate the finding, however, were not successful, and within a few years the claim was rejected.[13]

On its face, it is extremely unlikely that any single gene could cause substance abuse. Individual genes typically code for individual proteins that then perform relatively simple functions, such as skin color, enzyme production, or structural proteins.

Substance abuse, on the other hand, is extremely complex behavior. It involves numerous cognitive, neuromuscular, and emotional processes, all of which must be carefully coordinated. In a study of genetically modified mice that were bred for either high or low consumption of alcohol, it was found that about 3,800 unique genes appear to play a role in drinking behavior.[14] The entire human genome contains about 30,000 genes, and it is likely that no fewer than 3,800 are involved in some aspect of substance abuse. While it stretches the imagination to think that this number of genes would ever coalesce under evolutionary pressure to forge addictive behavior, it is preposterous to think that a single gene could be responsible. Nevertheless, this has not kept Noble from marketing a test for his "addiction gene."[15]

Let us accept that the twin and adoption studies are detecting something genetic that is related to substance abuse. The most plausible explanation is that the studies have uncovered a genetic correlation—a trait or group of traits that are shared by some or perhaps many substance abusers. It does not have to be shared by all, just shared often enough that its frequency is "greater than by chance alone."

As students of logic know, correlation is not causation. Two traits can correlate but have no direct connection to each other. A nation's stork population might increase the same year the human birthrate increases—a definite correlation—but the two are unrelated. Correlations can also be related but still not have a cause-and-effect relationship. This occurs when both are influenced by some external variable. The number of shark attacks at the beach highly correlates with ice cream sales at concession stands—a consistent finding every year—but the two are related only because both are dependent on the same external variable: hot weather.

The genetic studies are likely pointing to the second type of correlation: the studies are probably detecting not a genetic trait that causes substance abuse but one that is frequently found in substance abusers. If so, it would be a trait that nudges some individuals toward substance abuse. One possible genetic correlation is a temperament or personality that is attracted to substance abuse. There is good evidence that this is the case. Some researchers have found that alcoholics—prior to their drinking careers—tend to be impulsive and sensation seeking. Others have shown higher rates of criminality in the family members of substance abusers.[16] I have noted in my clinical practice—and in my family—that the eventual substance abusers were the ones most willing to test limits; they were also the most restless and impulsive.

On the Minnesota Multiphasic Personality Inventory, there are at least three personality scales that can predict, with greater than 80 to 90 percent accuracy, who is a current substance abuser. These are based on questions that do not address substance abuse directly; rather, they address certain temperamental traits and other risk-taking behaviors.[17]

I know one man who comes from a long line of substance abusers. He is risk laden and thrill seeking like his relatives, but he is not a substance abuser. He has cultivated the habit of mountain climbing. He describes a profound natural high each time he ascends a summit. He takes in the view with a deep feeling of accomplishment. I have no doubt that at such times he is tweaking his brain's reward center just like his relatives do with alcohol and cocaine.

The significance—or nonsignificance—of genetic correlations can be illustrated with another example. Consider the relationship between height and playing basketball. Human height is highly genetic. Most basketball players are tall. Twin and adoption studies would very likely show that basketball players have a relatively higher frequency of first-degree relatives who also play basketball—more frequently than what would be found by chance alone. This does not prove that playing basketball is genetic. Tall people are not destined to play basketball or any other sport. It implies only that tall people tend to gravitate toward the game because they have a competitive advantage over others. Claims that substance abuse is genetic should be taken as seriously as claims that playing basketball is genetic.

Habits, Genes, and Neuroplasticity

Focusing on whether genes control behavior misses the bigger story in genetic research over the last several decades. This is the story of how behavior controls genes—part of the emerging field of epigenetics. It is now well known that both environment and behavior can control gene expression, leading to profound changes in the structure and function of the body.

Genes lie on tightly wound chromosomes that are embedded with clusters of proteins. These clusters used to be considered "junk DNA." It is now known that they play important roles in regulating access to genes. One example of how the environment controls genes is good parenting. It has been shown that when mother rats lick, groom, and nurse their pups, they actually are opening access to a stress gene (the "glucocorticoid receptor gene promoter") in their offspring. This gene codes for important stress receptors so that good mothering helps pups soothe themselves when placed into stressful situations. Pups lacking this mothering have fewer glucocorticoid receptors to help them through hard times and instead display helpless and depressed behaviors.[18]

In other rat studies, exercise was shown to turn on genes coding for brain-derived neurotrophic factor, a protein that increases cell growth and augments connections that coordinate muscle control. Exercise thus turns on genes that help rats become more athletic. In another experiment, rats exposed to an enriched environment (toys, whistles, bright objects, wheels, and wooden houses) were compared to rats from an unenriched environment (a simple tray with shavings). In the enriched group, the protein coarctin, which is important in neuronal growth and forming more brain connections, increased fourteen-fold after only two days of training. In the unenriched environment, there was no increase.[19]

Epigenetics appears to mediate neuroplasticity, which is the process of forming new connections between brain cells. As one writer put it, neuroplasticity is "the discovery that the human brain is as malleable as a lump of wet clay not only in infancy, as scientists have long known, but well into hoary old age."[20] Neuroplasticity is why the brains of piano players are thick and intricate over regions governing fine motor control. This allows for efficient and almost unconscious movement of the fingers. The extent of neuroplasticity directly correlates with piano-playing ability. In addition, merely *thinking* about playing the piano—visualizing the movement of fingers several hours a day—produces brain changes within one week approaching those induced by actually moving one's fingers over a keyboard.[21]

Another example of neuroplasticity is what has been found in London taxi drivers who must master a complicated compendium of the city's streets prior to being licensed. In one study,[22] the MRIs of taxi drivers' brains were analyzed and compared with those of control subjects who did not drive taxis. The hippocampi (the brain region that governs spatial memory and navigation ability) of taxi drivers were significantly larger than those of control subjects. In addition, hippocampal volume correlated with the amount of time spent as a taxi driver.

The study showed, again, that neuroplastic changes occur in response to environmental demands.

Even when the brain is damaged through stroke or trauma, it can recover much of its previous functioning. Through mental force and physical practice, new brain connections can grow around areas of damage. Brain cells can also change their assignments. It has been shown that cells once reserved for registering visual experiences, for example, can help record auditory experiences if the eyes cease to function. Stroke patients have been known to regain the use of limbs that were once thought to be hopeless.[23] Experiments in mice have confirmed these findings. In one study, mice that were genetically engineered to have poor memory and small forebrains had both defects largely reversed after consistent exposure to enriched environments.[24]

Epigenetics and neuroplasticity appear to confirm William James's observation of a hundred years ago that "the phenomena of habits in living beings are due to the plasticity of the organic materials of which their bodies are composed." Genes do not cause substance abuse; substance abuse causes genes to reinforce substance-abusing habits. The good news is that stopping substance abuse will cause genes to reinforce habits of sobriety.

The practical application of current genetic knowledge is this: tell a substance abuser that his behavior is genetic—that he cannot control himself—and he will likely develop whatever neuroplasticity is needed to make substance abuse part of his limited lifestyle. On the other hand, tell a substance abuser that he can control himself and treat him like you expect as much, and he is likely to cultivate whatever neuroplasticity is necessary to practice moderation and self-control.

"Just Like Other Diseases"

The third common argument used to support the disease model is that addictions mimic many physical diseases: their course is hard to control, they do not always respond to treatment, and they are marked by frequent relapses. According to a cover story in *Newsweek*, "The addict's brain is malfunctioning, as surely as the pancreas in someone with diabetes."[25] In congressional testimony advocating mandatory insurance coverage for addictions, Representative Patrick Kennedy (D-RI), Congress's leading advocate for all things related to mental health and addictions, declared, "So if you had diabetes and you don't produce enough insulin . . . no one holds it against you. . . . But God forbid you have a dopamine imbalance in your brain that causes you to use alcohol or drugs."[26] And one researcher noted in a prestigious NIDA publication, "To see that alcoholism and addiction are chronic diseases, you just need to look at the high rate of recidivism."[27]

The obvious problem with this argument is that it is no argument at all. It requires an a priori acceptance of the disease model. The just-like-other-diseases argument is a debate over just what kind of disease it is. Is it one that doctors can fix on the spot, like removing a wart, or is it one that is chronic and difficult to treat, like diabetes or cancer?

Human behavior that is characterized by chronic recidivism does not argue for calling such behavior a disease. Consider serial killing and thievery. These also have relapse rates that mimic diabetes and cancer, but "treating" them like diseases would almost certainly result in higher rates of such behavior.

CONCLUSION

The disease model of substance abuse is a classic example of paradigm science. The available empirical science does not compel adoption of this model. Instead, the science demonstrates the resourcefulness of the human body. At the very least, it shows that our brains do not control us as much as we control our brains.

The next two chapters examine the addiction treatment industry, which started long before neuroscience was able to image and study the brains of substance abusers. And while what we know from brain science today does not support the disease model, the brain science of the 1950s and 1960s was even less able to support the disease model. But this did not stop the medical community from claiming early on that substance abuse is a brain disease and that treatment for it is effective. Without any science to support such statements, the industry was forced to rely on pseudoscience, and it guarded itself against criticism by demanding strict ideological conformity.

7

DECONSTRUCTING REHAB

Quitting a drug or alcohol habit is not easy. Most addicts have structured their lives around drugs and alcohol. They have limited their social contacts mostly to other users, they have alienated their families, and they have poor work habits, if they work at all. They often become moody, demanding, and irritable. Substance abuse becomes a way of life.

There is a lot of drama associated with quitting, but it should not be overplayed. Nicotine, for instance, is considered one of the most habit-forming substances known, yet the American Cancer Society says that there are an estimated 44.3 million *former* smokers in America alone.[1] Most former smokers have quit with no outside help.

Drug rehab enjoys widespread support from both the medical profession and the general public. The press routinely reports high success rates and often profiles first-person accounts of how rehab has been instrumental in changing lives.

Rehab's appeal is reinforced by its early observable gains. For instance, when rehab pulls addicts off the street, it forces a physical healing process that results in weight gain, the healing of skin rashes, and the return of normal menstrual and sleep cycles. With forced abstinence, the human brain dismantles the neuroplastic changes that led to craving, withdrawal, and tolerance. Addicts become friendlier as their moods stabilize.

Early in the history of addiction treatment, doctors were disappointed to learn that this initial physical healing did not prevent relapses. In the Yale Summer School lectures, the chief justice of the Connecticut Supreme Court used to say that he knew of criminal inebriates who were committed to institutions for thirty years and who on release were drunk within hours.[2] Clearly, something other than a healed brain is needed if one is to remain sober.

Accurate numbers are hard to obtain, but early impressions from experts within the field were not encouraging. While the press, for instance, had trumpeted success rates at the Yale Plan Clinics of over 80 percent,[3] Dr. George Vaillant reported that the alcoholics under his treatment programs had relapse rates above 95 percent.[4] Dr. Herb Kleber, who worked at the old Lexington Narcotic Hospital, noted that relapse rates for heroin addicts were over 90 percent within thirty days of release.[5]

As drug rehab has evolved, relapse rates have remained high, but now addiction experts consider relapses to be part of the disease.[6] Researchers have been forced to abandon them as outcome measures. They now examine levels of drug use. Any reported decrease in use is considered a sign of treatment effectiveness. The next chapter reviews these studies and shows that even with the bar set low, it is still highly debatable whether rehab has an overall positive effect, and I present several reasons why it might have an overall negative effect.

REHAB'S THEORETICAL FOUNDATION

There are two major assumptions behind addiction treatment. One is that addicts have biological and psychological deficits that predispose them to substance abuse. It does not matter whether addicts are born this way (because of a genetic predisposition) or acquire these abnormalities (through the effects of drugs). The purported deficiencies can include a lack of biological substrates that make sobriety possible, a lack of knowledge about drugs and health issues, a lack of self-esteem, or deficient interpersonal skills (such as an inability to resist peer pressure).

The second assumption is that addicts want to stop but cannot. Try as they might, they are unable to overcome the deficits or forces that lead to drug use. A corollary assumption is that if they do not appear motivated to change, it is because they are in denial or their disease is so advanced that they cannot think rationally. This is why many experts advocate involuntary rehab.[7] If addicts appear resistant, the assumption is that after spending time in rehab, they will become motivated when they begin to see the benefits of treatment.

THE COMPONENTS OF REHAB

To address these deficits, drug rehab has evolved to include some combination of psychotherapy, education, spiritual renewal, and medication. Below is a summary of each that will lay the groundwork for an expanded critique of rehab.

Psychotherapy

Talk therapy is delivered through group and individual counseling. Group sessions often resemble Alcoholics Anonymous (AA) meetings in that experience sharing is a big part. These sessions usually depart from AA, though, in that the members often confront each other in an effort to expose dishonesty and denial. Individual counseling usually takes the form of cognitive-behavioral therapy, where trained therapists help addicts make connections between thoughts and behavior. Faulty perceptions and hidden dynamics are thought to predispose addicts to self-destructive behaviors. Family therapy is also a common ingredient and is usually geared toward exposing relationship dynamics that contribute to substance abuse. Most addicts enjoy this kind of work; it is meaningful, and they like the repartee with learned therapists.

Education

Didactic sessions in rehab address individual drugs of abuse, the health consequences of substance abuse, and important aspects of the disease model. Classes also include instruction on nutrition, communication skills, and relationship issues. Education can address any need unique to the clients in the program. In the Washington, D.C., Superior Court Drug Intervention Program, for example, clients work through various modules that include "Ethnic-Specific Contributions to Civilization" and "Identifying and Changing Patterns of Criminal Thinking."

Spiritual Renewal

This typically includes some form of AA's twelve-step model. Almost all treatment programs incorporate twelve-step meetings within the program or require participants to attend meetings on the outside. These steps incorporate key principles from the Protestant religious tradition, such as believing in a higher power, turning one's life over to God ("as we understand Him"), taking a moral inventory, admitting wrongs, asking God to remove character defects, making amends to others who have been harmed, and taking this message to other addicts. In essence, the steps teach humility, personal responsibility, commonsense wisdom, and community outreach.

The twelve steps not only provide a road map for inner change but also are an important avenue for new social connections among those most likely to have burned through previous ones. And the spiritual dimension provides a template for important transcendent values. AA's reliance on anonymity and commitment to avoiding controversy helps "place principles before personalities."

Individuals who have been court ordered to attend rehab are often required to attend a minimum number of meetings per week; sometimes daily attendance is required for up to ninety days.

Medications

Three types of medications are approved by the U.S. Food and Drug Administration for addictions: replacement therapies, anticraving medication, and blocking drugs. I summarize each type below. More details can be found in appendix B.

Anticraving Drugs

Craving is the subjective experience of desiring a drug. The Food and Drug Administration has approved many different drugs for this purpose. Their effects are subtle, if they exist at all. Most doctors do not find these drugs to be very useful in practice.

Replacement Medications

These drugs are similar in chemical composition to drugs of abuse, but they induce less intense highs and are prescribed under controlled supervision. Examples include methadone for heroin addiction and the nicotine patch for a smoking addiction. Methadone has helped some addicts lead stable lives and avoid criminal activity. The problem with these drugs is they do not typically function as replacements; they are usually consumed *in addition* to the drugs of abuse.

Blocking Drugs

These drugs completely block the euphoric experience of getting high. Currently, there are two: naltrexone (ReVia), which blocks heroin and other opiates, and disulfiram (Antabuse), which blocks alcohol. These drugs have the distinction of being the most effective drugs in the world—and the least effective. They work 100 percent of the time if you can get addicts to take them. The only addicts who seem to benefit from naltrexone are lawyers, doctors, and nurses who are ordered to take the drug under threat of losing their professional licenses.

Rehab is delivered in a variety of settings. Inpatient rehab typically lasts three to six weeks and is the most expensive because it tends to be hospital based. Long-term residential settings cost less but last longer—up to a year or more. In these, patients live in group homes while attending meetings that are scheduled around employment or group chores. Outpatient programs run day or evening sessions while patients live at home.

Some treatment programs discourage medication use, which they believe enables the kind of chemical-dependency thinking that got people into trouble in the first place. While AA does not take an official position on medications (they officially avoid all controversies), many AA members look askance at the use of medications.

Programs typically develop their own unique approaches. The Phoenix House, the nation's largest long-term residential program, acknowledges that while addicts benefit from examining the psychological roots of their addictions, real change is about new values, attitudes, and skills. The Phoenix model pushes vocational training and education to prepare for life after treatment.

Disease model critic Stanton Peele, PhD, has developed the Life Process Program. He teaches that addicts should not view themselves as powerless, which is a major tenet of the twelve-step model, but should see themselves as powerful agents capable of making sound decisions with their lives.

The Minnesota model views substance abuse as a multimodal illness and relies on a multidisciplinary collaboration of professionals: addiction counselors, physicians, psychologists, social workers, clergy, and other therapists.

THE REHAB EXPERIENCE

Most addicts, especially those who have been homeless or on a downward spiral, find rehab to be an agreeable experience. It is a comfortable and safe reprieve from the harsh and risky world of drug abuse. The former addicts who are my patients in prison consistently say that they enjoyed their many trips through rehab. They knew that their lives were out of control, and they appreciated the fact that there was a safe place to regroup.

Rehab starts as soon as addicts walk through the door. They immediately encounter the authority and prestige of medical science. They see posters of brain scans. They notice disease model literature on day-room tables. As withdrawal symptoms wane and heads clear, addicts find themselves in a different universe. They encounter well-dressed, devoted professionals waiting to help them. They see advanced degrees hanging on walls, and they notice that staff exhibit unwavering positive regard. There are few demands other than to attend evaluations, counseling sessions, and recreational activities. Meals are served hot, rooms are kept clean, and counselors hover with a disarming friendliness. Staff members are often former addicts themselves, with the shared experiences speaking "the language of the heart," a concept borrowed from AA.[8]

Addicts undergo comprehensive medical, psychiatric, and social work evaluations. These are vehicles that connect addicts to a wide range of services: medical treatment for the many ailments they bring to rehab, mental health treatment for those identified as having mental health disorders, and then housing, welfare, and social services for the transition back to the community.

It is not lost on addicts that special financial arrangements are made for rehab. This is not the way things are handled on the street, where strict market forces in the form of cold, hard cash are required for every good or service. In rehab, patients are visited by reimbursement clerks who will submit billing on their behalf to insurance companies (if the addict is insured) or to state or federal sources (if the addict is not insured).

Treatment programs always elicit feedback. In fact, they are required to do so by the Joint Commission, the agency that certifies all health care organizations. Treatment centers typically have a complaint process and/or satisfaction questionnaires. The Joint Commission even has its own hotline and email address for those not happy with their care.

Not everyone stays to the end of rehab. Dropout rates vary from 20 to 75 percent,[9] but those who stay in treatment tend to show the most motivation and enthusiasm. They often say that they learn a lot about themselves and that they are glad to meet people who seem to understand them. Addicts develop new story lines; the disease model gives them an explanation for why they behaved the way they did. Graduation from rehab is a time of optimism and new commitments.

CHALLENGES TO THE THEORETICAL FOUNDATIONS OF REHAB

The Controlled-Drinking Controversy

Along the way, the rehab industry faced several significant challenges. One was the controversy over controlled drinking. A British study[10] reported that a number of alcoholics had returned to normal social drinking following rehab. Some clinicians had actually begun to use behavior therapy to teach addicts how to drink responsibly. A joint National Institute on Alcohol Abuse and Alcoholism (NIAAA) and RAND study[11] in 1976 found that up to 22 percent of alcoholics were drinking responsibly eighteen months after treatment.

The controversy was so big that it earned a segment on CBS's *60 Minutes* in 1983. Controlled drinking, it turns out, is anathema to the disease model. If alcoholics are able to return to responsible drinking, then perhaps they were not "allergic" to alcohol after all, and maybe it was always just an issue of controllable behavior. In addition, some claimed that it was irresponsible to teach alcoholics to drink responsibly because it would send the wrong message to the many other alcoholics who were convinced that they needed to remain abstinent.

While this controversy still continues in academic circles, it has largely become a mute point in the treatment community. Because of high relapse rates, rehab programs advocate neither abstinence nor controlled consumption; rehab teaches that relapses are part of the disease and that addicts need to be committed only to staying in treatment.[12]

Motivation

Another major challenge has been the issue of motivation. Are addicts like the rest of us in that they could change if they really put their minds to it, or arc thcy so impaircd that motivation is mcaninglcss? The disease model, of course, supports the latter. Addicts are said to change with treatment, not with motivation. The prestigious Institute of Medicine claims that appeals to motivation are "inconsistent with understanding the complex multiple factors involved in addiction."[13] Indeed, if substance abuse is a brain disease, there is no logical reason to place any expectations on addicts.

The problem, though, is what to make of the many addicts who quit on their own. In 1992, the NIAAA[14] found that 71 percent of a large group of former alcoholics were no long drinking abusively, and 75 percent of this group had received no professional treatment and had never even attended an AA meeting. We also know that the vast majority of servicemen who were addicted to heroin in Vietnam came home and gave up the habit with no professional help.[15] These examples indicate that motivation may be more important than many people think.

Dr. Alan Leshner, former director of the National Institute on Drug Abuse, once attempted to clarify the issue of motivation:

> One might ask where voluntary drug-taking behavior ends and the compulsive disease of addiction begins. And can't addicts talk themselves out of this craving? The answer is "no." By definition, an addict suffers from compulsive, uncontrollable drug craving and use.[16]

Leshner appears to be saying that those who quit on their own really were not addicted in the first place. This is a common belief among thought leaders in the field. It arises not from scientific research but from the disease paradigm.

Philosopher Sir Karl Popper explained the difference between a scientific theory and a statement of faith. He maintained that for a theory to be scientific, it had to be susceptible to being falsified.[17] He used the following to illustrate: the theory that "all swans are white" should be discarded if it is shown that black swans actually do exist. If the proponents of the theory, when faced with such evidence, declare that the black, long-necked birds really are not swans, then the all-swans-are-white theory approaches the level of a metaphysical statement. The theory is no more than a convention or statement of belief.

The theory that addicts cannot quit on their own has been falsified. And we know that those who quit are no different physiologically from those who do not quit. The only difference appears to be, as we discussed in chapter 6, greater motivation in those who do quit.

Loss of Control

Laboratory research has shown that when alcoholics are given alcoholic drinks but think that they have been given nonalcoholic drinks, they do not display out-of-control drinking, nor do they typically act intoxicated.[18] Such findings argue against the existence of a biologically based loss-of-control problem and point instead to the power of personal expectations. Other research has shown that addicts will decrease their consumption in order to earn rewards, even when they are experiencing craving and withdrawal symptoms.[19]

Anyone who has lived or worked with addicts will notice the selective nature of how, where, and when they consume their drugs. Drug consumption is always done surreptitiously and only in friendly environments. Addicts will delay their use until the setting is right. And addicts exert a tremendous amount of effort to avoid being detected: they try to act sober in public, they hide their drugs and paraphernalia, they try to keep the taillights functioning, and they can string together a coherent set of lies to keep others in the dark.

To most people, such behavior indicates not loss of control but over-control. According to the advocates of the disease model, being out of control is merely an expression of how far the disease can commandeer human volition. This is, of course, another nonfalsifiable assertion.

In June 2011, the Global Commission on Drug Policy issued a report that included this important fact: of the estimated 250 million drug users worldwide, only about 10 percent use drugs in an addictive or abusive manner.[20] This argues against a loss-of-control phenomenon and may point to the effectiveness of cultural controls since many Third World countries do not provide rehab networks for their substance abusers.[21]

THEORY VERSUS REALITY

The theory that addicts are deficient is universally shared by proponents of the disease model, but it is not readily borne out by the lives of addicts. Even the notion that substance abuse is driven by deep-seated, psychological conflicts is problematic. First, it does not distinguish between addicts and nonaddicts since almost everyone has deep-seated conflicts. In addition, I have met many addicts who are psychologically quite healthy. They are completely comfortable with their lifestyles and evince no apparent conflict or desire to change.

Even if we hauled every addict into rehab, there is no guarantee that the lessons will get absorbed or utilized or will have any long-term effect. In fact, after working with hundreds of addicts, I am convinced that addicts do not change their lives until they have sufficient quantities of this one factor: motivation.

Since motivation is so important in all other areas of human activity, it is hard to avoid dealing with in rehab. Taking their cues from the disease model's thought leaders, rehab counselors will tell addicts that motivation is required to stay in treatment, not for staying sober.

Despite all the posturing about deficits, complexity, genetics, and neurochemistry, addiction treatment still turns out to be little more than subtle appeals to motivation. Calling attention to the health consequences of substance abuse is an appeal to one's sense of self-preservation. Teaching the twelve steps is an attempt to help addicts find new meaning in their lives. Pushing cognitive-behavioral psychotherapy is an attempt to make addicts see that substance abuse is immature, impulsive behavior.

As the Institute of Medicine claims, appeals to motivation are inconsistent with the disease model. This is why when treatment programs make this pitch, it is done with the kind of forcefulness that only a psychoanalyst could love: discrete, nuanced, and encased as a thought experiment. While this tack might work for sober, reflective people, it is really no match for addicts as they wildly careen through life.

THE UNINTENDED CONSEQUENCES OF REHAB

While the disease model is appealing to science-minded people, it results in important unintended consequences. Placing addicts into the sick role increases the likelihood of continued drug abuse by 1) generating powerlessness and dependency, 2) generating a sick-role mentality, 3) bestowing transfer payments and social benefits, 4) connecting addicts to the mental health treatment industry, and, finally, 5) shielding addicts from the social pressures that are actually capable of motivating change.

Powerlessness and Dependency

One of the first things addicts absorb from most rehab programs is that they are powerless over their addictions. This is the only tenet of the twelve-step philosophy that I think is flawed. Nevertheless, rehab lowers the bar in many other ways. Addicts are taught that relapses are part of the disease and that they are responsible not for staying sober but for staying in treatment.

So entrenched are these ideas that one addict told me, on the occasion of his tenth hospitalization for substance abuse, "My treatment hasn't worked yet." This captures one of the most important unintended consequences of the disease model—the passivity and dependency of the sick role. Rehab can create a dynamic that views quitting as so complicated that many come to view it as not worth trying.

The Sick Role and Self-Fulfilling Prophesies

Sociologist Talcott Parsons argued that when a person is labeled "sick," he enters a role of "sanctioned deviance." He is released from the normal expectations of life. The only expectation placed on a sick person is to pursue treatment.[22] Since substance abuse is said to be a lifelong disorder, sanctioned deviance can become a lifelong phenomenon.

When people adopt the sick role, they begin to change how they think about themselves. In an influential paper, sociologists Paul Roman and H. M. Trice[23] argued that labels change one's self-concept to the point where the assigned behavior begins to be carried out. People begin to socialize with others who share their labels. The label becomes an identity badge.

The pernicious effects of labeling are well known to educators. It is called the Pygmalion phenomenon.[24] Labeling affects children's self-esteem, lowers expectations, and puts them at risk for self-fulfilling prophesies. Studies have shown that if normal children are randomly divided into two groups at the start of the school year and teachers are told that one group is gifted and the other is not, those who are labeled "gifted" will score higher on academic performance tests at the end of the year.

An Expanding Smorgasbord of Social Benefits

Another important consequence of rehab is how it serves as a gateway to an ever-expanding menu of social services. The disease model's central premise of helplessness greatly expands the number of services that addicts are said to require.

The National Institute on Drug Abuse illustrates this web of services in figure 7.1. It is a state-of-the-art treatment model for substance abusers. To the extent that substance abuse is viewed as a disease, society can expect to provide these services.

Addiction experts fail to see the unintended consequences of this kind of wraparound care. They believe that the services they provide

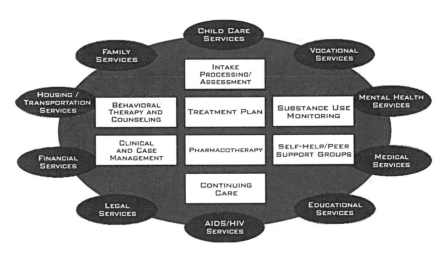

The best treatment programs provide a combination of therapies and other services to meet the needs of the individual patient.

Figure 7.1. The National Institute on Drug Abuse's vision of treatment services for substance abusers. Source: National Institute on Drug Abuse, *Principles of Drug Addiction Treatment: A Researched-Based Guide*, NIH Publication No. 99-4180 (Washington, DC: National Institute on Drug Abuse, 1999), 14.

empower patients and move them along a continuum from dependency to independency. Consider this statement from one expert in a methadone treatment facility:

> The clinic staff works with patients to formulate treatment plans that address patients' problems in order of urgency, such as criminal justice, mental illness, housing, employment, and education. As the first set of problems ease, the staff implements new services for the next most serious until, eventually, the cumulative improvement eliminates the need for most services.[25]

This is nothing more than paradigm-driven optimism. People with self-indulgent habits will always welcome services, but no one should make the mistake of thinking that this is the way to foster independence in this population. Among the addicts I have known, the more services they receive, the less they begin to do for themselves. It is no different from any kind of long-term welfare: it traps people into states of dependency.

Mental Health Disability

Another service that promises to spin out of control is the growing connection between substance abuse and the mental health industry. This is the movement called "co-occurring disorders" or "dual diagnosis." It focuses on people who have both substance abuse and mental health problems. The federal government's Substance Abuse and Mental Health Services Administration has developed the Co-Occurring Center for Excellence, which is currently providing Co-Occurring State Incentive Grants to develop the state infrastructure to provide comprehensive services for substance abusers.[26]

The American Psychological Association says that at least half the people who seek help with addictions have mental health disorders.[27] These estimates are underestimated, as they depend on diagnosticians acting conservatively. In practice, mental health providers apply their labels liberally. They typically view any emotional disturbance—and there are many among the addict population—as evidence of mental illness. The profession's diagnostic bible, the *Diagnostic and Statistical Manual of Mental Disorders*, can be painted as broadly as the ideological reach of the provider using it. Send addicts through mental health clinics, and the manual will have a "diagnosis" for every emotional perturbation that addicts experience.

Addicts with co-occurring disorders soon qualify for Social Security disability, Medicare, case managers, and welfare benefits to include housing assistance and food stamps. Addicts often spend years bouncing between psychiatric hospitals, rehab centers, jails, and subsidized housing in drug-laden, urban neighborhoods. In the past, disability benefits were paid directly to addicts and would go straight toward drugs and alcohol. When state officials realized that this was happening, they began requiring case managers to control cash benefits. Not to be outdone, substance abusers quickly learned that petty theft and drug dealing provided ample cash for drug purchases. When arrested, criminal charges are frequently dropped or pled down if defendants check into rehab.

The Loss of Embedded Cultural Controls

Perhaps the biggest drawback of addiction treatment is the way that control of the drug problem has been professionalized. I make the case in subsequent chapters that the drug problem will not be controlled until we deprofessionalize it. The only way to truly help addicts is to subject them to the values, expectations, and disciplines of the lay, working-class culture. Unlike professionals, laypeople are not inclined to support the disease model. They are inclined to hold people responsible for their behavior, which would incentivize addicts to start changing their lives. Unfortunately, laypeople rarely question the scientific community, so in the case of substance abuse, they take a backseat, and society loses its only hope for change.

CONCLUSION

The medical profession has created a drug treatment industry that has received little if any scrutiny. Stripped to its core, rehab is little more than ideological indoctrination into the disease model. At the margins, there are subtle appeals to practice sobriety.

In the end, there is nothing uniquely medical or technical about drug treatment. The brain will heal in any drug-free setting, and one would be hard pressed to argue that addressing motivation—subtly or not—requires advanced degrees in psychology or medicine. Furthermore, I believe that the thought experiments that addicts are asked to ponder during rehab are inconsequential when faced with the compelling incentives and disincentives they encounter in the real world.

The transformation from an out-of-control addict to a responsible user or abstainer is personally profound and can never be imparted. The drive or motivation that is required to make this change usually requires deep personal pain or conviction. There is nothing about rehab that forces this kind of tough decision making.

That said, it is important not to confuse rehab with organizations that have legitimate roles to play for substance abusers. I am referring, of course, to AA and Narcotics Anonymous (NA). Even though these are often incorporated into rehab programs or are imposed on addicts by the courts, the essence of the twelve-step philosophy is decidedly noncoercive and nonmedical. Members of AA and NA understand that people can change only themselves. These programs do not work on addicts; rather, addicts work these programs. AA and NA are where addicts go after they have gone through the ringer, experienced deep personal pain, and decided to change their lives.

Advocates of rehab point to outcome studies that appear to show that rehab really works. The next chapter examines these studies and reveals that, like rehab, the reality is different than the hype.

RETHINKING THE EFFECTIVENESS OF REHAB

The objections that have been raised about the disease model and drug rehab will fall on deaf ears if rehab actually works. And this appears to be the case, according to treatment outcome studies. The treatment industry has been trumpeting its successes ever since the days of the Yale Plan Clinics. Treatment is said to cut down on drug use, save money, and reduce crime.[1] The press routinely reports these claims, and lobbyists present them to legislators when pressing for expanded rehab services. A close examination will show, however, that these studies have huge methodological flaws and are capable of generating positive results even if none exist. A review of basic research and statistics will explain how this happens.

PRINCIPLES OF EXPERIMENTAL DESIGN

In pure experimental research, scientists test the effectiveness of an intervention by keeping all variables constant except the one to be tested. For instance, if researchers want to determine what dose of sunlight maximizes a plant's growth, they would start with a group of genetically identical plants and give each the same soil, nutrients, temperature, and water. Some plants would then be assigned to receive no sunlight (the control plants), and the others would receive varying amounts of sunlight (the experimental plants). At the end of several weeks, one could be fairly confident that differences in the health of the plants would be due to differences in the amount of sunlight they received. If all the plants turned out to be equally healthy, one would conclude that sunlight did not affect the health of the plants.

Pure scientific studies of human behavior are impossible to conduct. Researchers simply cannot control all the variables that influence people's behavior. When addicts attend rehab, for example, they are exposed to a wide range of personal, family, and social pressures. Friends and family members will express attitudes—positive or negative—about treatment. New relationships and even romances start in treatment. Addicts may have personality conflicts with their assigned therapists, and some may not warm to the religious aspects of the twelve-step philosophy.

Drug treatment is also not a linear force like sunlight. Rather, treatment is a hodgepodge of psychological exploration, education, peer pressure, skill building, value adjustments, and spiritual persuasion, all of which are experienced differently by those exposed to them. Unlike plants, people have minds of their own. They are not compelled to absorb anything. Some will sit through rehab with skepticism or boredom. Others go through the motions only to satisfy family members or probation officers. Still others soak up treatment. They believe and affirm everything about it and display a high degree of motivation to change.

Given the inability to control some or all of these variables, outcome studies may not be measuring the effects of treatment as much as surveying the lives of people who have attended treatment. Regardless, there are a number of common statistical features in these studies— four examined here—that can make treatment appear to be effective even if it is not.

Treatment Selection Factors

Selection bias is a prominent part of these studies. Treatment programs typically are made up of people who have come forward seeking help. Some degree of improvement might be expected months later even if this group receives no treatment at all. People come forward for help when their lives are spinning out of control or they are hitting bottom. These are effective motivators. This is why outcome studies must include a control group made up of people who have come forward seeking help but receive none. The control group could be assigned to either a sham treatment (such as meeting weekly to talk about stress) or to a no-treatment group (they are not seen at all). If the outcomes of the control groups are as good as those who receive treatment, one would have to conclude that the pretreatment motivational factors, rather than treatment, were the cause of any improvement.

Self-Reports

In 1998, the Government Accountability Office (GAO) reported that all major addiction treatment outcome studies have relied on self-reported data that "may overstate treatment effectiveness."[2] Substance abusers notoriously underreport drug and alcohol use, not necessarily because they are lying (which they frequently do) but also because of denial—a self-psychological technique to convince oneself and others that things are better than they really are. Addicts often lead pathetic lives, and they are forever seeking approval both from themselves and others. Survey them in the morning, and you will hear that they are no longer using. They are always in the process of quitting—until the evening's next debauch. Survey them a year after treatment, and they are likely to say that things are going well even if they are not.

Another factor is that former patients may want to report favorable results because they had positive feelings about treatment and they do not want to disappoint the surveyors, who they may view, rightly or wrongly, as emissaries of rehab. In addition, substance abusers often are mildly paranoid. If they think that the surveyors have any connection to law enforcement agencies, they will be more likely to report that they are drug free and following the law.

Interestingly, there are times when addicts are known to *overreport* their substance use: when seeking admission to treatment programs. This is especially true if they are homeless and winter is approaching. Addicts learn early in their careers that if their circumstances sound dire, they are more likely to receive services.[3] Prospective outcome studies often obtain their initial baseline data when addicts are applying for treatment. This combination of overreporting at the start of treatment and underreporting at follow-up can make treatment appear to be effective even when it is not.

Follow-Up Selection Factors

Another selection bias is the pool of former patients who agree to do follow-up surveys. After addicts go through treatment, some will be doing better than others. If outcome studies end up surveying mainly those who are doing well, it will give the false impression that treatment is more effective than it really is.

In outcome studies, former patients are usually offered cash (in the range of, say, $10 to $40) to answer questions about posttreatment life. Most take the cash and answer the questions. Others refuse to participate. Many others are never located, and still others will have died. Nevertheless, judgments about treatment effectiveness are typically based on the responses of those able and willing to be interviewed. These may in fact be only those with the best outcomes. Those who refuse to be interviewed, who cannot be located, or who have died may be those with the worst outcomes. The end result is that outcome studies tend to survey those who are doing relatively well.

The Cohort Phenomenon

Chronic substance abusers go through natural cycles. For instance, they often ride "benders" that last for weeks or months and that typically end in personal, family, or legal crises. Immediately after the crises, there is often a return to moderation or sobriety for months or even years because of either fatigue or the many social and environmental changes that crises bring. In most cases, a relapse is waiting down the road, but the point is that substance abuse waxes and wanes over the course of a lifetime.

Most addicts enter treatment at the height of these crises—either on their own or because of pressure from families or the courts. Thus, six or twelve months later—just when outcome studies start sending out surveyors—there is a good chance that many substance abusers will be doing better simply because they are in the moderation phase of their cycles. They are part of a cohort whose cycles are aligned and are being surveyed when they are doing relatively well.

OUTCOME STUDY: THE CALIFORNIA DRUG AND ALCOHOL TREATMENT ASSESSMENT

Let us examine several prominent outcome studies that illustrate these issues. One famous study is the California Drug and Alcohol Treatment Assessment (CALDATA).[4] Published in 1994, this research surveyed a large group of former patients who had participated in state-funded alcohol or drug treatment. Researchers attempted to contact 3,055 former patients and found 1,826 willing to be interviewed and who had been out of treatment for an average of fifteen months. Participants answered questions regarding four areas of their lives: substance use, health status, criminal activity, and employment. They were asked to give this information retrospectively for two different time periods: for the twelve months prior to entering treatment (baseline) and for the twelve months prior to the interview (follow-up).

Not surprisingly, the former patients reported improvement in all four areas from baseline to follow-up. In addition, the improvements were so great that researchers declared that for every $1 that taxpayers spent on addiction treatment, they got a return of $7 because of lower long-term costs to society. The researchers stated that, "the dramatic benefits to taxpaying citizens mostly reflects a 42 percent drop in the costs of crime."[5] Between the two time periods, the former patients reported a 93 percent drop in the use of weapons or force to commit crimes and said that they were involved in criminal behavior only for an average of 1.1 months during the follow-up period compared to 5.6 months during the baseline period.

To calculate the dramatic cost savings to taxpayers, CALDATA researchers calculated the average costs to society of a single crime and extrapolated this across the criminal activity that was reported during the two time periods. The CALDATA results were so impressive that they were reported in a front-page story[6] in the *New York Times* to bolster support for addiction treatment. And these results are still touted before state and federal legislators when lobbyists are making the case for more taxpayer support of rehab.[7]

The flaws in this study are hard to miss. For one, it did not include a control group. The follow-up pool also was not random but consisted of only those who agreed to be interviewed. The biggest flaw, however, is that researchers relied on self-reports for the data that produced the whopping seven-to-one savings: self-reported criminal activity. The researchers did not even check police records to determine whether the self-reported data were valid or in any way correlated with official records. And that would be hard to know anyway because not all crime is reported, and many reported crimes produce no arrests. The researchers simply accepted what the former patients said about their criminal activities.

Being fully aware that self-reported data might have compromised the results of the study, the researchers noted in a footnote that, "we minimized underreporting [of drug use and criminal activity] by carefully selecting and training interviewers in nonjudgmental but probing interviewing techniques."[8]

After working for many years in this field, I can assure you that there are no interviewing techniques that can reliably elicit the truth from former or current addicts. The uncritical acceptance of "probing interviewing techniques" in particular and of the CALDATA study in general appears to be an expression of profound faith in the work of the scientific community. It is similar to the widespread press coverage given the Research Council on Problems of Alcohol in the 1930s and the Yale Center in the 1940s and 1950s. Society appears to want to uncritically accept research findings as long as they come from the scientific community and as long they support a popular paradigm.

OUTCOME STUDY: DRUG ABUSE
TREATMENT OUTCOME STUDIES

Another famous study is the Drug Abuse Treatment Outcome Studies (DATOS). This was a large, multisite study funded by the National Institute on Drug Abuse (NIDA) that started in the 1990s. DATOS was the third large-scale NIDA-funded outcome study. The first was the Drug Abuse Reporting Program during the 1970s, and the second was the Treatment Outcome Prospective Study during the 1980s.

DATOS began with 10,010 clients who were interviewed twice during admission to ninety-six different treatment programs in eleven different cities from 1991 to 1993.[9] The clients were paid $10 to $15 per interview. The programs included outpatient methadone treatment, long-term residential treatment, outpatient treatment, and short-term inpatient treatment. Forty-eight percent (4,786 out of 10,010) of the clients were then randomly selected to be interviewed again twelve months after treatment ended. At follow-up, 557 were determined to be ineligible because they were incarcerated or were in hospitals that did not permit interviews. Of the remaining 4,229 clients, 74 percent were located. Of these, sixty-four were deceased, and another 117 refused. In the end, 70 percent (2,966) of the follow-up clients were successfully interviewed one year after treatment. A subsequent five-year follow-up study[10] was also completed using this same pool. At the five-year point, only 1,618 out of the 2,966 were located, and of these, 1,393 were interviewed because some had died and others had refused.

The intake and follow-up interviews asked clients to recall their behaviors for the preceding twelve months. The intake interviews collected information from the twelve months before they entered treatment, and the follow-up interview collected information for the twelve months preceding each collection point. The behaviors surveyed included drug use, criminal activity, health status, sexual behavior, and employment.

The results were amazingly positive across all four modalities of treatment and across both collection points. Weekly cocaine use among those in long-term residential treatment, for instance, dropped from 65.4 percent prior to treatment to 18.2 percent at the one-year point and 26.0 percent at the five-year mark. Among the outpatient group, weekly cocaine and marijuana use dropped by half at the one-year mark but were climbing toward the pretreatment baseline at the five-year mark.

Predatory criminal behavior decreased by over 50 percent in all treatment groups across both collection points. A subsequent study[11] examined the cost–benefit ratio for such a drop at the one-year follow-up for 502 cocaine-dependent clients. Treatment costs were estimated for two programs: long-term residential and outpatient. As in the CALDATA study, the tangible costs of crimes were also estimated. The cost–benefit ratio was estimated at 1.68 to 2.73 for long-term treatment and from 1.33 to 3.26 for outpatient treatment. That means that for each $11,016 that was spent for an episode of residential treatment, the savings to society in lower crime costs were up to $30,092. Likewise, for outpatient clients, each $1,422 spent on an episode of treatment resulted in a lower crime cost of up to $4,638. The authors noted that the positive returns on investments found in the CALDATA study had been replicated in DATOS.

But the limitations with this study are the same as with CALDATA: there were selection effects at all collection points, there was no control group, and all the outcomes were based entirely on self-reports.

OUTCOME STUDY: PROJECT MATCH

Another important study was Project MATCH, a $27 million effort funded by the National Institute on Alcohol Abuse and Alcoholism

(NIAAA) that reported its first results in 1997. This was a long-awaited project within the treatment community. It was believed that if individual patients could be matched to the right kinds of therapy, then better outcomes would be seen. As the journal *Science* noted in 1987, "It has become clear that much treatment research fails to find differential effectiveness because different types of patients have been clumped together in study populations."[12]

In Project MATCH, 1,726 alcoholics were recruited from nine treatment facilities throughout the United States. Before entering the study, the patients underwent eight-hour screening interviews that collected extensive clinical and demographic data. Patients were then randomized to three different treatment settings: twelve-step facilitation (TSF, which is based on the precepts of Alcoholics Anonymous [AA]), cognitive-behavioral therapy (which helps patients make connections between thought patterns and behavior), and motivational enhancement therapy (which encourages patients to increase individual responsibility and set goals and keep them). In the TSF and cognitive-behavioral therapy groups, patients were to receive twelve weekly therapy sessions. In motivational enhancement therapy, they were to receive three monthly sessions. In all, the patients attended about two-thirds of their sessions and were reassessed up to twelve months posttreatment.

The good news, according to the first NIAAA press release, was that all treatments showed consistently positive results. "The striking differences in drinking from pretreatment levels to all follow-up points suggest that participation in any of the MATCH treatments would be associated with marked positive change," claimed Thomas F. Babor, PhD, the principal investigator for the Project MATCH Coordinating Center.[13] The bad news was that the matching hypothesis was not confirmed; all patients, regardless of their backgrounds, did equally well across the different treatments.

The limitations of this study were profound. There were no control groups, and the outcomes were based on self-reports. The participants were also a self-selected group of volunteers. According to addiction expert Stanton Peele, Project MATCH included only motivated, stable, non–drug-using and noncriminal participants—the very people who would be expected to have the best outcomes.[14]

Critic Jeffrey Shaler told *Science News* that Project MATCH revealed that the most effective therapies for alcoholism are no more effective than "old time religion" (AA or TSF). He said that the idea of selling therapy for alcoholism alongside free self-help programs such as AA was like selling water by the river.[15]

Several years later, the Project MATCH story became more interesting. As it happened, Project MATCH *did* collect data on a no-treatment control group, but it was not included in the official release of the study. There is a reason for this: those who came forward for treatment but dropped out before their first sessions did as well one year out as those who completed twelve weeks of treatment. The data were published independently in 2005 by Robert Cutler and David Fishbain of the University of Miami.[16] They obtained an official copy of the Project MATCH data and reanalyzed it. Their conclusion: "Ineffective treatment would be the most parsimonious explanation for the rather surprising main findings of Project MATCH."

OUTCOME STUDIES WITH DRUG COURTS

One type of treatment setting that has shown some effectiveness is that connected with the criminal justice system. Drug courts, as they are commonly called, began in 1989 and are often funded by U.S. Department of Justice grants. They are growing in popularity, and today there are about 2,000 in operation.

There are two types of drug courts: deferred prosecution and post-adjudication. Participants are typically volunteers who attend regular treatment sessions and then appear in hearings before judges. Drug courts usually limit participants to those with nonviolent crimes, though it is common for participants to have prior criminal records. Progress is monitored by self-reports and/or random drug tests. In both settings, successful completion of a one- or two-year program typically results in dropping of the charges (deferred prosecution) or suspended/deferred sentences (postadjudication).

Another GAO report[17] in 2005 reviewed these programs and identified 117 outcome studies published between May 1997 and January 2004. The GAO selected twenty-seven evaluations that met "criteria for methodological soundness." The average number of previous arrests per participant ranged from one to about thirteen. Program completion rates varied from 27 to 66 percent.

The outcomes of drug court programs were predictable: those completing the programs showed lower rearrest rates within one year of entry—about ten to thirty percentage points below those of demographically similar arrestees who did not enter drug courts or who started treatment but dropped out. Reconviction rates showed reductions from eight to twenty-one percentage points. When mandatory urine drug tests were used and when this approach was combined with regular status hearings before judges who issued consistent sanctions for dirty urines, significantly more participants were drug free.

These results may not be as great as they appear because there still are prominent selection effects. Typically, only the most motivated defendants or those with the best attitudes are the ones who volunteer for or are given the drug court option. And those with the most motivation are the most likely to complete the programs. Furthermore, drug court participants typically face punitive sanctions if they use drugs during treatment. According to the NIDA, research "has shown that combining criminal justice sanctions with drug treatment can be effective in decreasing drug abuse and related crime."[18] While this sounds promising, it doesn't necessarily mean that treatment works; it might mean that arm-twisting works.

Indeed, an Urban Institute study in 1998 compared three types of drug courts in Washington, D.C., and the group with the best outcomes had received no formal treatment at all but instead experienced consistent sanctions for dirty urines. This group did better than the addicts who received intensive treatment with inconsistent sanctions.[19]

TREATMENT OUTCOMES: HOW DO WE MEASURE SUCCESS?

For drug treatment to be successful, it must directly affect subsequent behavior. Given all the competing influences that human beings face, this is a highly dubious proposition. Life is lived on the ground, so to speak, and the influence of ideas once contemplated during treatment sessions is completely dependent on whether these ideas are embraced and forced onto the real-life exigencies of the moment.

Let us assume for this discussion, though, that rehab does have a connection to subsequent drug behavior and that substance abusers really are trying to stay clean. How should we define treatment success?

When state inebriate asylums were first constructed in the nineteenth century, taxpayers and legislators had high standards for success. This was necessary because the general public was skeptical about treatment and had strict principles regarding the use of tax dollars. Professor Sarah Tracy has noted that in Massachusetts in the 1800s, they measured success by holding a job and being self-supporting.[20] Modern measures of success, on the other hand, are based on how addicts answer posttreatment questionnaires. There can be little doubt that the bar has been lowered. If we applied the nineteenth-century standard, we might have a different impression about the efficacy of addiction treatment.

THE FINANCIAL COSTS OF REHAB

Given what we now know about rehab, some might be interested to know what it is costing us. While an entire book could be devoted to this topic, I briefly summarize it here. Direct federal spending on drug rehab rose from negligible in the early 1950s to $9 billion in 1986 to $21 billion in 2003 and is projected to increase to $35 billion in 2014.[21] Public financing amounted to 77 percent of the total in 2003 but is expected to climb to 83 percent by 2014. "Private" funding is composed largely of state insurance mandates. As of 2009, forty-five states have insurance mandates for alcoholism treatment, and thirty-four states have mandates for drug abuse treatment.[22] On the research side, the NIAAA will spend $455 million in 2010 on alcoholism research, and the NIDA will spend close to $1.1 billion on drug abuse research.

The largest costs, though, are connected to ancillary benefits, such as welfare, housing, and "co-occurring" disability benefits. The Americans with Disabilities Act enshrined substance abuse as a bona fide disability, and in the 1990s the Social Security Administration began to award disability payments to individuals for nothing more than being an alcoholic or drug addict. The GAO reported in 1994 that 250,000 drug addicts and alcoholics were getting disability benefits at a cost to taxpayers of $1.4 billion every year.[23] Congress subsequently changed this practice by requiring that substance abusers have some other psychiatric disability before qualifying for benefits. As I argued earlier, this is no more difficult than getting substance abusers to walk into mental health clinics.

These costs, though, are about to explode. The rehab industry is like a freight train that has not even left the station. According to the U.S. Department of Health and Human Services, in 2009 only 11 percent of the 23.5 million persons aged twelve or older who are said to need treatment for a drug or alcohol problem actually received it. Twenty-one million people who are said to need rehab have not yet entered the system.[24]

This will soon change. President Obama's signature legislation, the Patient Protection and Affordable Care Act, will extend health insurance to 95 percent of all Americans. The act mandates comprehensive substance abuse treatment services for all covered persons.

CONCLUSION

The most charitable judgment to be made about the current system of drug rehab is that it has not been shown to work, at least in large outcome studies. And it is hard to see why anyone would expect it to work. Drug users *like* to get high, even if doing so causes problems for them. Like everyone else, addicts are heavily influenced by the environment around them. Since rehab is moving toward a comprehensive system of care, addicts who are exposed to rehab might become even less likely to feel the need for hard decision making in their lives.

So what are we to make of the people who seem to benefit from traditional rehab? I think the most likely explanation is that the same forces that send people to rehab are the forces that make people reexamine their lives: family crises, legal problems, health consequences, and so on. Going to rehab correlates with improvement, but rehab probably does not cause the improvement. The improvement comes from the pretreatment motivational factors that force people into treatment. This is analogous to a type of correlation discussed earlier. Shark attacks correlate with ice cream sales, but sharks do not cause people to buy ice cream. Both increase during the summer months because each is a consequence of hot weather.

This is why rehab outcome studies must include no-treatment control groups. When they do, as in Project MATCH, we should not be surprised to find that the controls do as well as those who attend treatment; both groups consist of substance abusers who are coming out of crisis points in their lives.

It is important to remember, also, that quitting is not rocket science. No one has to go to rehab to learn how to quit because addicts quit all the time. Substance abusers frequently go through periods of self-imposed sobriety to satisfy other goals. Some do it when they become physically exhausted and need rest; others do it because they have qualms about how they are living, and for others it is when families issue ultimatums. One addict told me that he remains drug free for days at a time whenever his widowed mother needs him to work on her house. His hands shake, but the sooner he finishes, the sooner he returns to his habit. Among those who quit abusive or addictive consumption, most do so with no outside help, according to the National Longitudinal Alcohol Epidemiologic Survey.[25]

Nevertheless, Mark Twain's quip that "quitting is easy, I've done it nineteen times" says much about the enduring strength of habits. The temperance-era and disease model–era insistence on abstinence, however, has probably created more problems than it has solved because it places unrealistic expectations on people. Moderation, on the other hand, is both a reasonable and an attainable goal.

The next chapter explores the habit model of substance abuse. The prescriptions that flow from it are quite different from those informed by the disease model because they are based on a respect for human nature. Professional rehab counselors do have a role to play under the habit model, but it is different in tone and substance from the work they do now.

9

THE HABIT MODEL

Reframing substance abuse as a habit may not seem particularly novel since we already refer to drugs and alcohol as "habit form-ing" and historically addicts have been called "habitués." Nevertheless, the habit model accounts for important observations not captured by the disease model, and it leads to a dramatically different response to the problem.

Others might think that a habit model trivializes the seriousness of the issue. After all, everyone has habits, and most of these involve little if any thought. Examples include how we laugh, how we get dressed, and what we do with the toothpaste cap. But not all habits are so quaint. Humans also have complex habits—the kind that develop over time and require concerted effort. Daily exercise routines, mastering a musical instrument, and complex assembly-line work are just a few ex-amples. Psychologist William James observed over a hundred years ago that the end result of habits is to "simplify the movements and diminish the conscious attention with which our acts are performed."[1]

Advocates of the disease model argue that substance abuse is a dis-ease because it makes changes to the brain. Yet all habits make changes to the brain, and when they do, they use normal, not diseased, physi-ological mechanisms. Habitual behavior makes neuroplastic changes because the brain always adapts to the demands that are placed on it. Expose the brain to regular doses of cocaine, and it adapts one way; ex-pose it to regular sessions of guitar practice, and it adapts another way. In each case, the changes are predictable and consistent.

When habits are stopped, those neuroplastic changes largely return to their prehabit states. Habits do leave footprints, however. Former smokers often return to multiple-pack-per-day habits if they start smoking again. Once-accomplished flautists—who have not played in years—approach their former playing levels within a short time after returning to practice.

In the case of diseases, we can assume that something has gone awry—an invading bacillus, a malformed collection of blood vessels, or the abnormal proliferation of cancer cells. Habits involve normal brain changes; diseases involve abnormal brain changes.

Substance abuse as a habit begins to capture the full complexity of addictive behavior. Habits develop because humans want to avoid discomfort and acquire pleasurable sensations. We also strive for efficiency. Successful habits bring positive returns on multiple levels—emotional, mental, and physical. Habits can assuage pain, relieve boredom, stimulate euphoria, provide a basis for self-identity, and even establish a career.

Consider the habit of regular visits to the fitness club. Physical exercise is much more than the sought-after release of tension at the level of skeletal muscle. The fitness club is an important venue for enhancing health and longevity. It also creates a social identity. Club members share a concern for health, diligence, and beautiful bodies. The club becomes a public stage for physical prowess and genetic endowment. The end result tweaks pleasure receptors in the brain throughout the day. Missing a workout can cause guilt and perceptions of disfiguration, all of which are relieved by redoubling one's efforts at the next visit.

Drug use has analogous dynamics. Not only does it satisfy a sought-after chemical experience, but the drug-using subculture is an important source of social identity. Entering it provides an instant connection with those drawn to the high-risk, fast-talking, counterculture lifestyle. During prohibition, drug use is an expression of independence. The illegal nature of it all merely enhances the "forbidden-fruit" effect. The cat-and-mouse game played with the police contributes to the intrigue. And if that is not enough, drug parties are typically fraught with promiscuous sex and wild displays of narcissism. The more risk laden the behavior, the more "cool" it becomes.

Habits like these cannot be reduced to the linear processes that are needed to fit the disease model. Habits satisfy too many dynamics and too many desires. It is for these reasons that habits also do not lend themselves to being "treated."

The good news is that people can change their habits, but they usually do so only when faced with compelling incentives. The kind of incentives that work will occupy the next few chapters. For now, I want to explore why incentives work and why what happens in the brain during substance abuse does not alter the importance of incentives. In truth, drug-induced brain changes act as incentives themselves, as will be shown below.

INCENTIVES

Environmental incentives are important in the management of substance abuse because addicts are already awash in them. Tell addicts that free drugs will be provided at a party, and every addict in town will be there. Addicts also respond to disincentives. If the police are parked in front of the party house, addicts will abruptly turn around and leave. They avoid unfriendly situations. You will never see addicts snorting cocaine in lobbies of police departments; they will wait until they are behind closed doors. Drug purchases, likewise, are conducted surreptitiously and will be postponed if conditions are unfavorable.

Perhaps the most compelling environmental incentives occur when addicts "hit bottom," the point where the costs of substance abuse finally outweigh its benefits. Ask any seasoned substance abuse counselor, and he or she will tell you that addicts do not change until they reach this point. Where this happens is different for everyone, but when it is reached, it becomes a highly effective antidote. This is consistent with the nature of habits: people practice them as long as they provide a return. When habits no longer deliver, people change them.

For many addicts, hitting bottom occurs when their children are removed from the home or when extended family cut off contact with them. For others, it is when they lose a job or a professional license. Harsh consequences serve as poignant wake-up calls and tap into rich troves of resourcefulness that are characteristic of human nature.

The disease model posits that substance abusers have lost free will—that there comes a point where the compulsion is so strong that addicts cannot resist. This has never been shown to be true but not so with its obverse: if you let substance abusers fall—and fall hard—almost all of them will change. Call it what you want, the concept of "hitting bottom" works. Recall Samuel Johnson's adage that the prospect of getting hanged in a fortnight wonderfully concentrates the mind.

Theoretically, society could lessen substance abuse by offering cash rewards for people to remain clean and sober. This might work in small, closely monitored settings, but it would never work on a societal level, as human nature would sabotage the program. More "addicts" would come forward than ever existed, and real addicts would take the cash and buy more drugs.

In the end, habits are opportunistic; they persist as long as their benefits exceed their costs, and those costs are not always understood by outsiders. It is easy to look at an alcoholic who has lost his family and his job and is now living at the homeless shelter and then assume that he has hit bottom. But you would frequently be wrong. Even among the dispossessed, there are robust social and interpersonal dynamics (shared social identity, shared grievances, romantic relationships, ongoing substance abuse, and so on) that form complex, personally meaningful communities.

This book proposes a set of cultural controls that significantly raise the costs of substance abuse. These controls are essentially disincentives. They do not rely on the medical or legal professions. They rely instead on laypeople—on the mores and disciplines of responsible, working-class people.

Laypeople have the power to control drug habits because they own—or should own—the most valuable social assets of any society. It is the hardworking, taxpaying, and child-rearing among us who control the homes, the warm beds, the meals, and the social contacts that connect people to jobs and opportunities. They also produce the sons and daughters who, as they enter adulthood, are sought by others for dating and marriage. Responsible people are found at every level of society. They control the goods.

When this group bestows these goods on those who act responsibly and withholds them from those who do not, it wields tremendous leverage over society's general level of civility. Responsible people can and should expect others around them to act similarly, just as they have had to do to get where they are. When faced with irresponsible behavior, responsible people need to cut off the goods. In this way, they create incentives for everyone to do the right thing.

The medical profession is not capable of moderating this kind of tension. It is not within its nature to administer sanctions, and it has its own habit of pathologizing irresponsible behavior. The lay culture, on the other hand, deals with these tensions on a daily basis. From the time that children are taught to pick up their toys, families have been shaping responsible habits. They know how to do it both by instinct and by tradition.

Since substance-abusing habits often do not respond to the kind and gentle persuasion that is characteristic of rehab, stronger disincentives have to be applied. Fortunately, there are two experiences that all human beings strive to avoid: shame and physical discomfort. These are avoided like the plague at every strata of society. Shame may be relative, but every social group has its rules that all members must follow or be shamed thereby. Physical discomfort, on the other hand, is absolute and must be avoided at all costs.

The effectiveness of these kinds of disincentives cannot be overestimated. Shame and physical discomfort are acutely experienced. I have seen shame work in small doses, such as a family deciding that Uncle Harry would not be invited to future holiday dinners because of his drinking. And it never takes too many nights sleeping on cold park benches for a twenty-year-old man whose parents have kicked him out of the house to learn that repeated acts of unruly behavior will have the same painful consequence.

Many people reflexively oppose the use of shame, as if it violates some higher moral standard. Yet shame is used throughout society and to good effect. Parents use shame to mold the behavior of their children ("What will your father think of what you just did?"). Coaches frequently use shame to shape the behavior of athletes, and politicians of all stripes can barely carry on conversations without referring to their political opponents' shameful policies.

Charges of shame help sharpen discourse. It puts people on the defensive, which is beneficial if it forces them to reexamine their behavior. Shame is also a great sign of respect—"You could have behaved differently, but chose not to; shame on you." It implies, at least, that the intended target has the capacity to act differently.

We would all benefit if we began to think of substance abuse as shameful behavior. In doing so, we would show respect for each other and reinforce what constitutes respectful behavior. Advocates of the disease model, of course, will oppose the use of shame—but only when used by others. They will use shame liberally when they hurl accusations of stigmatization.

NEUROPLASTIC INCENTIVES

As shown in chapter 6, all habits make changes to the brain, reflecting the brain's attempts to acclimate to the demands that are placed on it. Flood the brain with drugs and alcohol, and the brain creates cellular sensitivities that are experienced as tolerance, craving, and withdrawal. Stop flooding the brain, and those sensitivities return to baseline. Based on what we know from neuroscience, it is probably more accurate to say that the brain does not control behavior as much as behavior controls the brain.

There is little doubt that drug-induced brain changes act as important forces for more drug use, but these are neither necessary nor sufficient. Drug highs are commonly pursued in the absence of craving or withdrawal, and those who quit cold turkey always do so at the height of such symptoms. While these changes will nudge users toward more use, they do not *cause* more use.

Craving and withdrawal symptoms essentially function as internal incentives. Whether they get satisfied depends entirely on how they stack up against competing incentives. A simple truth is this: addicts who get their basic physical needs met, such as regular meals and a comfortable place to sleep, or who are protected from experiencing any shame for their behavior will face fewer incentives to change their ways.

WHEN INCENTIVES DO NOT WORK

There are some substance abusers who seem to be unaffected by adverse consequences. They repeatedly consume drugs or alcohol to the point of poisoning and near-death experiences. They have lost so much that there is nothing left to lose. "Hitting bottom" has lost meaning. These addicts seem to function outside the parameters of normal human habits.

Substance abusers who have reached this stage are not satisfying habits as much as tempting fate. They are either suicidal or testing the limits of their own perceived invincibility. Both types usually end in early deaths; one by choice, the other by accident.

Chronic substance abuse frequently leads down this road. Addicts burn a lot of bridges as they plod through life. Family members can only take so much lying and stealing before they sever ties. Addicts acquire long police records. They have poor work histories and explosive personalities and are unpredictable. Even their drug-using friends will steal from them and eventually abandon them. Self-indulgent habits are one-way tickets to existential demise.

It should be pointed out that addicts do not usually reach this point without having had a lot of enabling in their lives. The interventions I propose in subsequent chapters will help prevent this dark journey primarily because they are administered early in the course of substance-abusing habits, long before people lose the will to live. Nevertheless, we have two options in regard to these types of addicts. We can take the laissez-faire approach, which is to watch them suffer and die, or we can use coercive measures to manage their lives. In chapter 12, I propose a benevolent way to do the latter.

HABITS AND THE REHAB INDUSTRY

Substance abuse counselors do have a role within the habit model, but they will have to give up the notion that they can "treat" addicts. Instead, counselors will need to acknowledge that addicts can only change themselves. This will be a difficult transformation for many professionals whose careers have been fueled by the disease model. The common belief within the industry, that addicts change only after they have had sufficient exposure to the ideas and words of rehab professionals, will not be easily discarded.

Under the habit model, drug counselors would become teachers and consultants. They could run seminars for addicts where they teach about the effects of habit-forming drugs; the neurobiology of the brain's reward system; how neuroplasticity creates craving, tolerance, and withdrawal; and how those changes are undone. They could teach about the power of expectations and the kind of lifestyle changes that are needed to become controlled users or abstainers. They could review laws regarding drug use and highlight what the consequences are for any misuse that harms others. What people do with this information, however, is beyond the reach of the profession.

Attendance at these sessions would be made up of addicts who wish to change their lives, addicts who have been given ultimatums by family members, or addicts who have been ordered by the courts. These sessions, though, would likely be measured in hours or days rather than months, and the marketplace would probably price them at several hundred dollars rather than the tens of thousands of dollars that traditional rehab costs in the government-protected, disease model market.

Drug counselors could also serve important roles as consultants to families who need to learn how not to be enablers but rather to learn creative ways to incentivize addicts. Counselors could also consult with employers to create and implement company policies that promote the safe and responsible use of drugs and alcohol.

Individuals and families, of course, would be free to pay for any kind of "therapy" that the free market supported. Some might want expensive spa therapy at exotic locations. Individual therapists could develop whatever programs attracted clients: traditional rehab, hypnosis, spirituality, psychoanalysis, New Age, and so on. With no taxpayer subsidies, though, all these would become boutique treatments, but they would all have their customers.

Both AA and Narcotics Anonymous would continue to exist and would not need to be modified. I expect that self-help programs might even become more popular than they are now. The only suggestion I have is that judges resist the urge to mandate attendance. Twelve-step programs are intended to be voluntary programs. That is how they were founded and how they function best in people's lives.

HABITS AND THE MEDICAL PROFESSION?

Since the consumption of drugs and alcohol does not involve diseased physiological processes, there is almost no role for the medical profession on the front end of substance abuse. The only exception is that doctors should warn their patients about the health consequences of substance abuse and, like drug counselors, teach their patients how habits develop and how they go away. But what people do with all this information, again, is beyond the reach of the profession. This is why discussions about substance abuse should be framed as political and cultural issues, not as medical problems. Bringing the medical profession into the debate has only derailed clear thinking on the issue.

The medical profession's most important role, however, is on the back end of the problem: treating the physical consequences of drug use. Examples include medically supervised detoxification from alcohol, barbiturate, or benzodiazepine abuse. Withdrawal from these substances can be complicated by seizures or other life-threatening conditions, such as delirium tremens. Other treatments will be needed for hepatitis, psychosis, HIV, tooth decay, skin abscesses, and lung and heart disease. Substance abusers, however, must bear the costs of these treatments. When others pay for treatment, substance abuse is being enabled. Only when addicts begin to feel the full costs of their behavior will physical consequences begin to act as disincentives.

CONCLUSION

Habits are a normal part of human nature. They serve legitimate human needs, and they will stay confined if they are accepted and embedded within a framework of informal cultural controls. Laymen have no interest in reinforcing bad habits, and addicts respond to incentives just as everyone else does.

The insistence on abstinence—whether based on the disease model or a moralistic perspective—stems from another kind of habit that is common to human nature: the desire to control others. If people give that up, drug users will lose one incentive for the in-your-face style of consumption that is common within the drug subculture.

10

THE CASE FOR DRUG LEGALIZATION

The current war on drugs represents the professionalized approach to controlling drug abuse. Law enforcement professionals strive to stop people from selling drugs, and treatment professionals attempt to keep people from consuming drugs. The federal government has formalized these two approaches as "supply reduction" and "demand reduction."

There are many reasons why drug prohibition does not work and other reasons why it should be repealed. One of the more important reasons to repeal prohibition is to ensure that all drug use occurs under a set of layperson-centered cultural controls. The professionalized, prohibition-centered approach ensures that drug use occurs outside cultural norms and sends those with unruly habits to treatment experts who coddle and enable them.

All societies attempt to minimize deviant behavior. In regard to drug use, Western cultures rely on education and appeals to health. Recall the popular 1987 poster, created by the Partnership for a Drug-Free America, of the egg in the frying pan with the caption, "This is your brain on drugs."

Educational efforts like these are effective for a large segment of the population—those who want to comply with social norms and who seek the approval of parents, elders, and teachers. In my experience, this group comprises about 75 to 80 percent of the population. It includes those who are devoted to healthy lifestyles and who often avoid legal drugs, such as tobacco and alcohol. They also avoid using prescription drugs outside the parameters set by their physicians.

But education is notoriously ineffective for the more rambunctious among us—the other 20 to 25 percent who seek to defy norms and expectations. They are attracted to the forbidden fruit. Being risk takers, they play roulette with their own health. They frequently push social boundaries and bamboozle others if they can get away with it. They are narcissistic and restless, preferring immediate over delayed gratification.

This is the subpopulation that is drawn to the substance-abusing habit. Education and appeals to health have little effect. In the end, this group responds only to consequences—the kind with teeth. They often have to "hit bottom" before they change their ways.

WHY PROHIBITION DOES NOT WORK

Drug prohibition laws are a perfect fit for the disease model but not for the way people live in the real world. People who use illicit drugs *like* to get high; they want their drugs. Sellers, likewise, want the lucrative profits that come from drug dealing. Prohibition laws are little more than abstractions or inconveniences to the voluntary participants in these exchanges.

Prohibition does not work in part because the amount of police intrusion that is required to effectively stop the flow of drugs would be unacceptable to most freedom-loving people. Search-and-seizure laws, while protecting fundamental liberties, also allow drugs to be transported with relative ease. And because of the high profit margins, for each drug dealer arrested, there are five more waiting in line. The criminal penalties are worth the risks for those accustomed to life on the edge. My patients in prison consistently confirm this. They tell me how easy it is to transport and sell drugs. More often than not, they are in prison for convictions unrelated to possession or delivery. Unfortunately, the more society tries to enforce prohibition, the more lucrative and intriguing the drug trade becomes.

Prohibition also fails because it enhances the forbidden-fruit effect. Consumption becomes a badge of independence. Substance abusers are not just drawn to drugs; they are drawn to *illegal* drugs. Tell some people that they are not allowed to do something, and they will do it as soon as you turn your back.

Prohibition creates incentives to overindulge. Efforts to avoid detection drive production toward more concentrated drugs and forces consumption into smaller time slots. Consumption is necessarily done on the sly with more dangerous substances. Nothing about prohibition fosters moderation. Even Marxists, who were never loath to remove rights and freedoms, understood this basic concept. Writing in the British socialist magazine in 1908, labor leader Harry Quelch noted that "experience has proved that any form of prohibition has but stimulated that worst form of the drunkard's vice, secret drinking."[1]

Prohibition, then, only gives the illusion of control. When the criminal justice system apprehends substance abusers, it becomes little more than a conduit for coerced treatment. And with all the ways that treatment enables substance abuse, the courts can become coercive enablers of the problem.

Several years ago, a felon on parole got admitted to my psychiatry ward after getting apprehended for unruly behavior that was a direct result of his renewed methamphetamine habit. In discussions with his parole officer, I learned that such individuals are rarely violated (sent back to prison for failing to stay drug free) "as long as they are getting the help they need."

I present this caveat not because drug use should be punished—it should not—but to illustrate that the present system of control is no control at all. We have pushed drug users away from civil society and sent them off to treatment professionals and court officials who seem to have drunk too much from the disease model. Attend a drug court hearing, and you will likely leave with the distinct impression that the therapists and judges are working harder than the defendants.

All of this brings up the drama associated with the current state of affairs. The drug subculture is marked by deceit, thievery, violence, sexual promiscuity, and rampant narcissism. Drug users become outlaws, and the demeanor they acquire instills fear in law-abiding neighbors and family members. Addicts happen to like this power, and they are not put off by getting arrested because they instantly walk into the sick role. When they continue to use drugs, they are said to be "struggling" or "relapsing." If they stay sober, they are "in recovery"—a precarious state anchored to the low expectations of the disease model.

The sad reality is that prohibition and the disease model have created this drama. Society really is working harder than substance abusers. Not only do taxpayers have to fund this show, but they get to live in crime-infested neighborhoods that are dangerous only because of prohibition-inspired illegal behavior.

There is a growing movement today that seeks to end prohibition primarily because of the violence and chaos it creates. The movement advocates a policy of "harm reduction," and one of its principal proponents is the Drug Policy Alliance Network in New York City. This George Soros–funded organization claims that "a harm reduction approach favors treatment of drug addiction by health care professionals over incarceration in the penal system."

Ignoring the false dichotomy that the above position presents, the hallmark of harm reduction is its heavy reliance on treatment. To be sure, ending prohibition would make society safer, but the next step would be disastrous. Further reliance on the health care industry would only enable substance abuse.

THE BENEFITS OF DRUG LEGALIZATION

Drug legalization would instantly remove the violence and corruption associated with the drug trade. Business disputes would be settled in a court of law rather than at the end of a gun. Consumers would not have to become outlaws, and everything they buy would have its purity and contents controlled. Average individual consumption would likely increase, but the loss of the forbidden-fruit dividend and new respect for personal responsibility would likely attenuate the consumption of the heaviest users. The public would also reap billions of dollars in new tax revenues and savings from not trying to enforce prohibition. Harvard economist Jeffrey Miron has calculated what federal, state, and local governments spend to enforce prohibition and what they fail to collect in taxes from the sale of drugs. He says the direct costs of prohibition are about $70 billion each year.[2]

The other important benefit of repealing prohibition—and the one that is most relevant to this book—is that, when coupled with the rejection of the disease model, we would completely deprofessionalize the drug problem, thereby subjecting drug users to the discipline of embedded cultural controls. Once laypeople realize that they have the power—and responsibility—to enforce standards of respectable behavior, they will take up the cause.

Doing so requires no special knowledge or training; laypeople will simply implement the kind of behavioral controls that work well in all other areas of human activity. This will translate into shame or physical discomfort for substance abusers, which is precisely what they will need to find the motivation to practice moderation. When responsible laypeople act to secure their own comfort and safety—by simply following their own self-interest—they will create a culturewide network of control.

EXPECTATIONS

One of the unintended consequences of prohibition laws is how the expectations that come with them promote intemperate behavior. Recall that these laws are based on the notion that drugs are dangerous; they are believed to take over the human will to resist them. Expectations like the "fried brain," loss of control, and "relapses are part of the illness" all contribute to the likelihood of self-fulfilling prophesies. The gravity of these expectations is profound: a core feature of being human—possessing freedom of the will—is said to be completely lost by consuming illegal drugs. Is it any wonder that many drug users behave as if they are wildly out of control?

The power of expectations was demonstrated years ago in research[3] where drinkers were given unlimited access to alcohol in a "tasting" test. They were served drinks that contained vodka but were told that they contained only tonic water, or they were served drinks that contained only tonic water but were told that they contained vodka. The results showed that for both alcoholics and social drinkers, subjects who expected to drink vodka (but received none) drank almost twice as much and acted more inebriated than those who expected to receive only tonic water (but actually received vodka).

Expectations do work in the real world. A sociologist once examined 17,500 arrest records in New York City's Chinatown from 1933 to 1949 and found that not one arrest involved public drunkenness.[4] Yet alcohol is a big part of that culture. The Cantonese emphasize self-control through strong family and community norms. Drinking is embedded within many cultural and religious practices, but they also rely heavily on shame and social rejection when faced with irresponsible drunken behavior.

Prominent addiction researchers Don Cahalan and Robin Room have noted that the ethnic cultures with the lowest incidence of alcohol abuse—the Jews and Italians—also have the lowest abstinence rates and the highest consumption rates.[5] This is made possible because both cultures embrace consumption within a framework of embedded cultural controls. Addiction researcher Stanton Peele writes[6] that the Jews promote moderation by rejecting the major components of the disease model of alcoholism.

The experience of Great Britain in the previous century is also instructive. In his book *Drug Crazy*, Mike Gray recounts how for most of the twentieth century, heroin addicts could legally obtain supplies of heroin from their family physicians. In doing so, they remained in good health and were usually employed, and their neighborhoods had low rates of crime. Getting heroin was legal and void of drama. When the British government changed course and forced addicts to get off heroin—no doubt, for their own good—crime, disease, and irresponsible behavior skyrocketed.[7]

Repealing prohibition laws would instill a whole different set of expectations: people can control their behavior, and if they act like they cannot, then they will face unpleasant consequences.

It is important to remember, too, that the dangers of drugs and predictions of out-of-control drug use tend to get exaggerated. Historically, this was done to justify stricter prohibition laws. In 1919, for example, in the aftermath of the Harrison Act and after doctors largely gave up prescribing the drug to addicts, the New York City health commissioner estimated that there were 103,000 heroin addicts in the city. To cut down on crime, the city set up clinics to dispense free heroin to users as young as fifteen years of age. Yet no more than 8,000 addicts could be located within the year.[8] Others have noted how intemperate users of drugs and alcohol receive a disproportionate amount of attention because they add "color" to history.[9]

CONCLUSION

Human nature is nothing if not resilient. People who are drawn to drugs and alcohol will behave like they are out of control if that is the expectation they live under and especially if they have enablers with the same mind-set.

In the end, the best way to control drug use is to embrace it and subject it to commonsense, informal, cultural discipline. Self-control rather than abstinence should be the expectation. In fact, society would do best not to focus on drugs and alcohol at all but to reinforce expectations about personal responsibility and respect for others. After all, excessive drug and alcohol consumption does not cause irresponsible behavior; rather, irresponsible behavior causes excessive consumption.

I propose a set of cultural controls in chapter 12 that have a time-tested heritage that worked to control substance abuse for much of recorded history. In the next chapter, though, I discuss drug use in children, which is an entirely different phenomenon. Children do not have the maturity to handle self-indulgent habits and must be shielded from them.

11

CONTROLLING
TEEN DRUG USE

Most habits start early in life. Childhood is the time to learn habits that lead to success in adulthood: a strong work ethic, emotional fortitude, a passion for education, and good social skills. Childhood is not the time to become derailed by self-indulgent habits, the kind fostered by the drug subculture: slothfulness, disrespect, lawlessness, deception, and anarchy. Children must be protected from these at all costs.

Even if drug prohibition laws are repealed, drugs should still be illegal for children, just as we currently do with alcohol. The only exceptions might be when parents decide to incorporate legal drugs into the family repertoire. A strong case can be made that children should be served wine during dinner and religious ceremonies and be allowed to consume tobacco under parental supervision. This removes much of the forbidden-fruit élan and allows children to practice responsible consumption. Mediterranean cultures have demonstrated that this approach works.

Outside of these exceptions, though, parents must completely block their children from becoming involved with drugs and the youth drug subculture. Currently, many children are slipping through the cracks. The most recent surveys show that almost half of high school seniors have used illicit drugs. While this figure has remained stable for several years, today's drugs are cheaper and more habit forming than those of previous generations. The use of crystal methamphetamine, for example, often turns into a habit after just a few uses, and a mere $20 can keep a teenager high all weekend.

Most children are not drawn to drug use. They are drawn to pleasing their parents and others in authority. Tell these children to avoid drugs, and they will follow your advice. Others are naturally self-protective and will figure it out on their own. Not all children, though, are so easily directed. These are the risk takers. They tend to be restless, show little remorse, and are attracted to the forbidden fruit. As with some adults, the more you talk about the dangers of drugs, the more this group wants to try them.

Regardless of the type of children you have, all of them will benefit from a no-nonsense style of parenting that is clear about expectations and just as clear about consequences. I encourage parents to create written contracts with their children starting in middle school. These contracts should spell out any behaviors that are prohibited and what the consequences will be. Contracts should also spell out desirable behaviors and what the rewards will be. These agreements should be modified regularly because incentives change as children age.

Typical punishments for substance use might include three to six months of being grounded, forty hours of community service, no use of the car, cell phones that only call home, and so on. If these consequences are explicitly stated ahead of time—and consistently delivered—many children will get the message and steer clear. But the most risk-laden teens will not be deterred. For them, the greater the punishments, the higher the risks, meaning that they will be enticed to use even more elaborate deceptions to evade detection.

It is especially for these children that I recommend the highly effective intervention of home-based urine drug testing. It breaks through deception, and children who do not use drugs are never offended, especially if they know to expect it. Interestingly, government antidrug agencies do not support home drug testing, and the medical profession is strongly opposed to it.

The idea that parents can or should drug test their children comes as a shock to many, which nicely illustrates the influence of the disease model. Society seems to have decided long ago that responsibility for keeping kids off drugs was a job for the experts. Parents seeking this control have had to overcome several roadblocks.

In 1996, officials at the Food and Drug Administration (FDA) tried to block the sale of home-based drug kits by claiming that they were too complicated for parents. They felt that parents would not know how to handle positive tests. In congressional hearings, Thomas J. Bliley Jr.

(R-VA) exposed the agency's "nanny state" mentality.[1] President Clinton supported[2] parents' rights to have these tests, and the FDA eventually approved them. The tests are now widely available on the Internet for as little as $2 (for a single-drug panel) to $7 (for a five-drug panel). And they are no more difficult to conduct and interpret than a home pregnancy test.

The American Academy of Pediatrics came out against home-based testing in a 2004 article[3] over concerns that testing might decrease "honest communication between parents and teens." The article also expressed concerns about "whether parents could ever obtain free, informed consent for drug testing from their own child." The academy recommended that a "professional trained in the interpretation of drug tests" supervise all drug testing.

The problem with this opposition—other than the obvious professional self-interest—is that no pediatric professional is going to be available at 1 A.M. when your daughter breaks curfew and is acting strange. You need to test her then, not a week later when you finally get an appointment. The communication concern is also a red herring: if parents tell their children in advance that they will be tested, the only issue of honesty is whether the parents are going to keep their word. If a test is negative (no evidence of drugs), then parents will have more reason to trust their child; if the test is positive, it can only open the door to more honest communication.

The Office of National Drug Control Policy runs a program called the National Youth Anti-Drug Media Campaign.[4] While the website contains useful information for parents, it steers clear of recommending home drug testing. Instead, it recommends taking your child to a health care professional. But if doctors are concerned about gaining informed consent, you are not likely to leave the clinic any wiser.

Home drug testing is best done as part of a comprehensive plan of protection. Parents should get to know the parents of their teens' friends. They should ensure that social activities have adult supervision, and parents should prohibit their children from socializing with known drug users. Parents should always provide structured supervised activities: sports, music lessons, volunteer work, employment, chores at home, tutoring sessions, and so on. Keeping children productive is very important for success. Families should also have their own traditions and customs that give children a sense of belonging. Regular sit-down family meals, a shared religious faith, connectedness with the extended family, and meaningful traditions around the holidays always give children a sense of belonging and significance.

Home drug testing gives teens a compelling excuse to resist peer pressure: "No thanks, my parents test me." More important, testing keeps children honest. Drug-using teens are notoriously dishonest and go to great lengths to deceive their parents. They often develop double lives: superficial compliance at home and school while they sink deeper into the drug underworld. Testing is the only technique that breaks through this deceit. When teens throw the trust issue in their parents' faces, parents should remind children that trust is always earned.

Teens respect parents who take this no-nonsense approach, especially if they know ahead of time what to expect. I know one young lady who cannot wait to be tested again because she knows her clean test will earn her a new outfit.

Parents hold the keys to keeping kids drug free. They should not be seduced into thinking that the task is too technical or would be better left to the "experts."

Below are two stories of adolescent drug use: one that is managed poorly and the other properly. These are composites of the many cases I have seen from my work in child and adolescent clinics, from talking to family members and friends, and from listening to the stories of the prisoners I treat, almost all of whom were substance abusers as teens.

HARD-CORE CORY

There was nothing in Cory's early childhood that would have predicted the path he took. He was an adorable toddler and was part of a large, close-knit extended family. He loved being the center of attention, which was not unusual for a firstborn.

Cory was fearless and risk taking. He would chase balls into the street without checking for traffic. He climbed higher than other children, and he was always drawn to the company of older boys, especially those given to pranks and anything that looked devious.

His parents divorced in grade school, and his father started another family in a distant town. Beginning in the seventh grade, when boys enter that awkward stage of growth spurts and self-doubt, Cory found solace by hanging out with a group of boys characterized by dark clothing and heavy metal music. They were cool. They smoked cigarettes. They hated school and made fun of jocks. They also smoked marijuana.

Marijuana was a badge of defiance, but it also provided a tranquil, agreeable high. Cory and his friends would smoke prior to the start of the school day. They would derisively laugh at the straight kids. They mocked their teachers and the slogans from DARE classes. Junior high became a smug haze.

Cory talked his mom into allowing him to spend most Friday and Saturday nights at friends' homes. When she questioned his plans or sought to coordinate those plans with other parents, Cory became angry and accused her of not trusting him. She found it easier to back down.

During these weekends, Cory would check in periodically and return Sunday evening. What his mom did not know was that Cory was spending weekends at young-adult party houses. Alcohol, LSD, ecstasy, cocaine, and marijuana were regular weekend fare. Since drugs cost money, Cory and his friends—being the youngest members of the crowd—were pressed into thievery and burglary. Shoplifting and car prowling provided the necessary fodder for pawn shop–funded weekends. Cory also pressured his mom into buying expensive coats, shoes, and jeans and then returned these items for cash. When his mother wondered what happened to the missing items, Cory fabricated stories about thieves. Sometimes she repurchased the items, only to see them disappear again.

Cory's grades dropped, and he became more hostile at home. In the ninth grade, Cory got caught shoplifting. Juvenile probation ordered drug counseling. By the tenth grade, truancy grew in step with a new methamphetamine habit, which provided such a physiological jolt that Cory, on the occasion of his first meth high, resolved that there was no greater experience in life.

Cory soon learned how easy it was to monitor movements in the neighborhood and break into homes when people were away. At age sixteen, he was caught and spent thirty days in juvenile detention. His parents hired an influential attorney who got the charges dropped on the condition that Cory attend drug rehab and complete one year of supervision. He learned to carry a vial of clean urine on him at all times. He was drug tested twice that year and passed both times. He graduated from rehab with flying colors. He knew what they wanted to hear.

He came to realize that thievery and burglary were too risky. Selling drugs was safer because both parties wanted a quiet, conflict-free transaction. Selling was also far more lucrative. Cory could support his drug habit and clear about $500 a week with no more than two or three deliveries. He learned from his mentors the economic value of a more aggressive approach to debt collection. He started to rough up those who were late with payments. His peers feared him. He wore expensive clothes and jewelry. He was able to buy gifts for his mom, who in turn placed fewer demands on him.

His drug habit grew worse. He lost weight and became paranoid. He started to think everyone was watching him. At the age of seventeen, he became acutely psychotic after a several-day meth binge. He was taken to the local psychiatric hospital, where he fought imaginary demons.

On discharge, he was again sent to rehab. This was a forty-five-day inpatient adolescent program in a rural ranch setting. His mother's insurance paid only half the cost of the $34,000 price tag. She took out a second mortgage for the other half. Cory actually enjoyed this inpatient experience. He knew his life was out of control. He ate and slept well, gained weight, played sports during recreation therapy, and took part in many other structured activities. He had meaningful moments with his mother during family counseling.

Cory and his peers did well in this program but not because they were being deceptive. They were teens, after all, so their optimism and invincibility were natural. The adults around them mistook this optimism for an embrace of the sober lifestyle. More accurately, these were risk-laden, experience-heavy drug addicts who were frolicking like kids. Rehab had become one more pleasurable experience. The tempo was upbeat, the catharsis was refreshing, and the boys and girls in the program quickly befriended each other. It was widely known, albeit unspoken, that Cory and his friends would not be sober for long.

Shortly after discharge, Cory resumed his drug habit. He did not fall back into it as much as he embraced it. It was what he knew. It was where he had power and influence. Sure, he had some ambivalence, but he knew he had a safety net. He was coasting smoothly when tragedy happened. During a contentious drug transaction, eighteen-year-old Cory became extremely paranoid and pulled out a gun and killed one of his customers.

Cory's family was devastated. They pooled resources to pay for a private lawyer. He still received a fifteen-year sentence.

Today, Cory sits in the state prison. At the age of twenty-three, he is sober, physically fit, and sane and has a job making uniforms. He is learning to play the guitar. He attends chapel services every week. He has spent two forty-day periods in solitary confinement after fighting off inmates who were pressuring him to join gangs. They leave him alone now, as most people do. His parents occasionally visit. His grandparents send Christmas and birthday cards. Naturally, he regrets the path he took. He blames no one but himself. He says that drug treatment was a joke. "Rehab doesn't make you quit. No one quits until they're ready. You have to want it. I didn't want it until it was too late."

MOODY MONICA

Monica was a shy, quiet young girl who did well in school but spent a lot of time in her room. She lived with an emotionally labile mother and a father who was distant and stern. Her parents fought often, and they seemed to be more tuned in to the needs of her two much younger siblings.

The family moved across town just prior to the start of high school. Monica felt isolated and inadequate. She had no friends, and none of the other students seemed to like her. Eventually, a group of students approached her. They were vibrant, outgoing, edgy, and cool. They brought marijuana and ecstasy to school. Monica decided to take the risks and try them. The drugs opened up a whole new Monica. Her friends liked her, and she got in touch with a wild, new part of herself. She began to tune out her parents.

It was her antagonistic behavior and falling grades that first raised red flags. After her parents found marijuana in her dresser, they followed the recommendation of the school counselor and took her to an adolescent rehab clinic. The experts concluded that she had a "co-occurring disorder." Monica was said to have a chemical dependency problem and a clinical depression that was related to the move. Toward the end of ninth grade, she attended a thirty-day treatment program, got on antidepressants, and seemed to be doing better.

After returning to school in the fall, she quit taking her antidepressant, refused to go to counseling, defied her parents, and wholeheartedly adopted the new dress code of her peers. She denied that she was using drugs. The school recommended taking her back to the mental health clinic, which they did, but Monica was unruly and defiant. The psychologist recommended that they consider another evaluation at the rehab center.

Monica's parents were looking for other ideas. Their daughter was at a crucial point in her development. At sixteen years of age, she was headed for disaster. The family had large out-of-pocket expenses for both rehab and therapy, and after the last round, they could not afford any more. They were also skeptical of her treatment. They knew the kind of girl she had been. Underneath the crust of defiance and lies, there was a confused but sweet young lady. They knew how much her new peer group influenced her. They began to believe that Monica's problems stemmed not from a brain disease but from being a typical adolescent. She had feelings of inadequacy and wanted to be accepted by her peers.

Monica's parents took action once they realized that an adolescent's feelings should never be allowed to run the show. They followed my advice to go to the drugstore and buy over-the-counter drug testing panels. They were to hold Monica at home until she submitted a specimen. I had warned them that Monica likely would put off the testing long enough to consume large amounts of water in the hope of diluting her urine. Just as predicted, she did not void for hours, but when she did, she tested positive for marijuana and cocaine.

It was not just Monica who had to change. Her parents realized that they too had to make adjustments. Their daughter had gotten into trouble in part because they had not been paying attention. They felt guilty. But they soon realized that Monica had a mind of her own. Even if they had done everything correctly, she still might have taken this path. Parents cannot take responsibility for everything a child does, but they can take responsibility for everything they do.

Monica's parents decided to redo the structure and routines of the family. They wanted to protect Monica, of course, but they also wanted to prevent this from happening to her younger brothers. They developed a comprehensive plan that completely insulated Monica from her drug-using friends. They withdrew her from the public school and enrolled her in a private religious school. They completely blocked all connections to her former peer group. They took away her cell phone and car keys and restricted access to the Internet. She was confined to home except for supervised school activities. She spent weekends with her parents working on home improvement projects, church functions, or community service activities. Her parents supervised homework during the evenings. She made friends at her new school but with the non–drug users. Monica did not have enough unsupervised free time to run with the druggies. She did not go out on Friday and Saturday nights except for outings that her parents or other adults supervised. For two summers during high school, she worked on her grandparents' farm.

Monica's parents gradually released her restrictions. She got a job during the school year, and they allowed her to have a boyfriend. They randomly drug tested Monica until she became an adult. She never again visited a rehab clinic. She also never tested positive again. Today, Monica thinks her parents might have gone too far, but she admits they did what they did because they love her. She also noted that her parents seemed happier as a couple.

HOW TO WRITE BEHAVIORAL CONTRACTS

There is no better way to structure a child's life than with a coherent, written plan in the form of a behavioral contract. These should be written no later than the start of middle school. This is the time when children are commonly exposed to drug and alcohol use and the time when many children start going astray. Contracts should be posted in a private part of the home that is not observable by guests who do not have a need to know.

While it is best to have contracts that are mutually agreed on, this is not always possible. Not all children will cooperate. If this is the case, parents should still write a contract and post it. Parents are the legal and moral authorities in their families, and their rules and expectations are not subject to a child's veto anyway. But if a child participates and feels like he or she has been part of the process, then he or she will have more ownership in the authority of the contract and a harder time disputing it.

Single parents, especially moms, often have difficulty with risk-laden teenage sons. It is best to have strong adult males—uncles, grandfathers, or pastors—present to validate and enforce written contracts. Most teenage boys respect only one thing: power. If you bring powerful men into a young boy's life, he will be much easier to control and will develop the requisite humility to succeed in life.

Children want to know the rules and expectations that apply to them. They also want to be protected. The reason many kids join gangs is that the rules are clear, disobedience is not tolerated, and they get the protection they crave. Children are drawn to this kind of power and clarity. Parents and teachers should take a few cues from gang leaders.

Contracts deflect many family conflicts. Parents are able to maintain more composure because they can redirect hostility onto that piece of paper—the contract. When children violate the contract, parents can say, "Oh, Jason, I'm so sorry. I was hoping that we wouldn't have to deliver this consequence but that contract forces my hand." Jason's anger can then be directed at the contract.

TIPS ON DEVELOPING TARGET BEHAVIORS

Behaviors should generally be listed in positive, desirable language. For instance, "Grades will be Cs, Bs, and As" is better than "No Ds or Fs." Another example: "Always be kind to your sisters" is better than "Do not be mean to your sisters." The negative formulation in this case leaves open the option of just ignoring his sisters, which is not kind. Better to be positive and kind since those are the attributes that parents want to instill.

The technological revolution has made parental monitoring more efficient and accurate. For instance, schools now have portals where parents can log on and see a child's day-to-day progress and current grades. Parents can also install GPS monitoring software (http://www.vehicle-tracking-gps.com) in their cars to track where their children have gone and how fast they traveled to get there. You can even have the system text you if certain parameters have been exceeded. Computer monitoring software exists (http://www.spectorsoft.com) to track which websites your kids have visited, the content of their emails, and text messages if delivered on the computer.

SAMPLE POSITIVE BEHAVIORS

- Make your bed and straighten your bedroom every morning before school.
- Take the car only to places where you have permission to go.
- Drug tests are always clean.

- All school assignments will be turned in on time.
- Always shows respect for Mom and Dad.
- Always performs scheduled chores.
- Always set an example for your younger brothers and sisters to follow.
- Always owns responsibility for personal behavior.

TIPS ON DEVELOPING REWARDS AND CONSEQUENCES

Rewards and punishments must be relevant and powerful enough to motivate. I do not recommend that rewards be too lavish. Obeying the rules, after all, should be an expected norm. Consequences should be sufficiently severe to act as deterrents ("Grounded for thirty days") without crushing the spirit of your child ("Grounded until you turn eighteen"). Not all consequences should be construed as punitive; many might better be viewed as character building, such as "Twenty hours of volunteer work at the animal shelter."

Punishments tend to work best if they reflect something a parent can control rather than compelling a child to act. For instance, "No cell phone for a week" is a preferred punishment over "Clean the living room every day for a week." The latter can set up a seven-day battle over trying to get your child in the cleaning mood. Parents want to make sure they are not working harder than their teens in fulfilling the obligations of the contracts.

Another example: if you want to check your children's homework, make sure they are responsible for bringing it to you rather than you having to ask for it. The contracts can list suitable consequences if children do not present their homework each night.

Remember that the most potent disincentives for teenagers will be whatever takes away their freedoms or connections to their peers: the car, the cell phone, the Internet, and being allowed to go out on weekends. It will not take too many times losing these privileges before you see marked improvements in their behavior. See table 11.1 for an example of an abbreviated behavioral contract for children.

A child's world is filled with positive and negative incentives. A parent's task is to be creative enough to see them. When parents do, they will be able to move their children in the direction they want them to go.

Table 11.1. A sample behavioral contract for children

Target Behavior	Time Frame	Reward	Consequence
Always be kind to your sisters	Every 2 weeks	One extra Netflix rental for the weekend	Loses video games for twenty-four hours for each infraction
Grades are C and above	Each semester	$10 per A, $7 per B, $3 per C	No sleepovers until grades are C or above
Clean drug tests	Each episode	None. This is expected behavior.	Grounded for sixty days. No cell phone and no Internet except for homework. Volunteer forty hours of reading time at the nursing home.
Completes all scheduled chores without being asked	Each week	Usual liberties on the weekend	Grounded for the weekend

Effective parenting often takes the form of President Teddy Roosevelt's maxim, "Speak softly and carry a big stick." Clear rules and tough consequences will maintain order in any home. Yelling or other displays of wild emotions are neither necessary nor helpful.

This is the value of written, behavioral contracts. They prevent confusion, enabling, and overreacting. They also avoid the inconsistencies of trying to establish rules on the fly. Teenagers have little emotional control, and they will look for cracks to exploit. Expect wild reactions from them, but do not retaliate in kind. Planning ahead, when things are calm, can prevent a lot of mistakes.

Delivering consequences for childhood misbehavior can be done with few if any comments. Let the "big stick" of preannounced consequences do most of the talking.

RECOMMENDATIONS FOR HOME DRUG TESTING

If parents choose to drug test their children, it is best to let them know this ahead of time. For most kids, it will act as a deterrent. Parents should specify that they reserve the right to drug test any time they want and that any refusal to submit a specimen will be treated like a positive test. While testing is important, it is not necessary to do battle with your child. If they refuse to cooperate, simply treat it as a failed drug test—as if they have been using drugs. This is how it is done in the adult workplace. Home drug testing gets kids ready for the real world.

Here is another dynamic you can weave into the testing: parents can offer a "reduced sentence" if a child confesses to drug use prior to the testing. If a child thinks the test will find him or her guilty, he or she will have an incentive to confess. If so, this would solve the problem of the occasional false negative (the child has been using drugs, but the level in the urine is low enough that it does not register). Offers like this are common in the criminal justice system; they are called plea bargains.

Sophisticated drug-using teens often use elaborate means to escape detection. Some will keep in their possession a vial of "clean" urine from a non–drug-using friend. Others will store a vial of clean urine in the bathroom—under the sink or in the ducts. If parents do not want to directly observe a child urinating into a specimen cup, then ensure that no clean urine is accessible. Do not let your child carry any items into the bathroom except the specimen cup you provide. When returned, the specimen should be warm and yellow. If it is cold or room temperature, it is not their urine. If it is colorless, your child may have anticipated the test and drank a lot of fluid to dilute his or her urine with the hope of coming in under the threshold. It is possible, too, that he or she filled the cup with tap water.

Many people—adults and children—have difficulty urinating under pressure. It is called "shy bladder." If this happens, reassure your child that this is a common problem. The solution is to relax as much as possible and wait. Have your child do homework or read while you wait with him or her. Do not let your child go to a friend's house. The bladder will need to empty eventually. Drinking sips of water can help.

When testing the urine, be sure to follow the instructions that come with your tests. Give your child a disposable testing cup and have him or her fill it halfway. Remove the test card from the sealed pouch. Pull the cap from the end of the test card and dip the strips into the urine to the level indicated (see figure 11.1). Immerse the tips for ten to fifteen seconds or whatever is recommended in the instructions. Replace the cap and place the card on a nonabsorbent flat surface. Generally, the results are read at about five minutes. All control lines should appear.

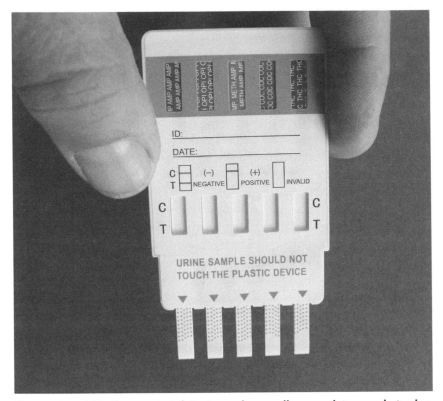

Figure 11.1. This five-way test detects cocaine, marijuana, opiates, amphetamine, and methamphetamine and sells for less than $5.

If there has been no drug use, all the test lines should also appear. If a test line does not appear, then it should be considered evidence that your child has been using that drug.

Be aware that some prescription medications can be detected on urine drug tests. If your child has been prescribed codeine for cough suppression, it can show up positive for "opiates." Sudafed and other cold preps containing pseudoephedrine can cause positive results for "amphetamines." But do not be taken in by claims that secondhand smoke was responsible for a positive marijuana test. The amount of secondhand smoke exposure that is required to turn the test positive is so great that your child should face consequences for spending so much time with pot smokers. The test does not turn positive by walking past someone who is smoking.

Home alcohol test strips are also available and are highly sensitive. They are technically similar to the drug tests except that you have your child spit onto the end of the test strip. At two minutes, compare it to the scale on the back of the package. Any color change indicates that your child has been drinking. A box of twenty-four costs under $40 (see at http://www.alco-screen.com).

Some children will try to sabotage alcohol tests by rinsing with Listerine when they get home. This will also produce a positive result, and they will use it to deflect the fact that they were out drinking. If you plan to test for alcohol, do it as soon as children walk through the door. Remember, do not argue or fight over this test. If your child fails to fully cooperate, treat it like a positive test.

WHERE TO BUY HOME DRUG TESTS

Home drug tests can be purchased at local pharmacies or online. You will pay more for tests at the drugstore, but they have the added convenience of being available the night you need them. If you plan ahead, you can order marijuana and alcohol saliva tests for under $2 each. Multiple-drug testing panels are available for slightly more but usually do not exceed $5 to $7 per panel.

There is great price variability on the Internet, but real bargains can be found, like those listed above. The following sites sell home drug testing kits:

http://www.drugalcoholtest.com
http://www.homehealthtesting.com
http://www.testcountry.com
http://www.testmyteen.com

A WORD ABOUT PARENTAL GUILT

Nothing can be as satisfying as rearing a child, but nothing is more prone to emotional pain. We all make mistakes in life, whether through miscalculations, carelessness, or getting derailed by our own addictive behavior. Life also forces us to make unwanted decisions, such as divorce or having to work far from home. When circumstances adversely affect children, parents often feel bad and respond in ways that can make matters worse, such as being too permissive or too angry.

When children are caught using drugs, parents often experience anger, guilt, shame, or all three. It is important to identify these emotions because parents react to them differently. Ideally, we would first identify our emotions and then plan a response. Instead, we usually react impulsively and with little thought. Only later do we notice whether we responded appropriately. This is not the best way to do things.

Feelings of guilt indicate that we have done something wrong. It usually involves something we could have done differently, such as having provided more supervision. Guilt means our children were hurt by our actions. Shame, on the other hand, is a more pernicious emotion. Shame indicates that we are concerned that our child has made us look bad in the eyes of others. Shame is a concern about our own image. Guilt is a concern for our children.

Research[5] indicates that when parents feel shamed by a child's behavior, they tend to react in maladaptive ways, such as yelling, using overly harsh discipline, or using inattention as a form of punishment.

Guilt, on the other hand, tends to result in reactions that are more adaptive, such as explaining why a behavior was wrong and how to behave more appropriately in the future.

Thus, guilt is much preferred over shame. Dealing with shame is beyond the scope of this book, but it requires serious self-examination and rethinking one's place and purpose in the world. Guilt, though, is very useful and should be used to motivate us. That said, we should not distort guilt and make it something other than a concern for our children. Some tend to exaggerate guilt when they have narcissistic tendencies: "I'm such a good parent; how could I have ever done such a thing?" Some enhance guilt by comparing themselves to others: "They're the ideal family; they never make mistakes."

The antidote to such thinking is to accept the fact that each of us is flawed—and deeply so. We all make mistakes with our children. If it appears that others do not, then we do not know them very well.

We deal with guilt by using it to force us to start doing what is right—today.

The serenity prayer applies here: "God grant me the serenity to accept the things I cannot change, courage to change the things I can, and wisdom to know the difference." The past cannot be changed, but the present can.

When parents experience guilt, they should examine the situation and change whatever will prevent it from happening in the future. Careful forethought and planning are key—hence the value of the pre-arranged contracts. Parents can even write down their own "standard operating procedures" to help them be consistent and think clearly when issues arise: "When Rebekah asks to spend the night at a friend's house, 1) check her contract to make sure she is eligible and 2) discuss it with the other parents before giving permission."

Parents should never lean on their children for emotional support, nor should they call attention to their mistakes or shortcomings. Parents can, however, admit their mistakes if children call attention to them and even when it might appear that parents are hypocrites. In truth, there is nothing hypocritical when you do the right thing for children: "Yes, I did drugs when I was your age, but it was a mistake. I wish people had structured my life like I'm about to do for you."

Kids will sometimes play the guilt card, but parents should stick to their principles: "It's okay for me to drink alcohol because I'm an adult. I've earned my way in the adult world. You're a child and haven't yet shown you can do the same. When you're an adult, you can drink alcohol too."

When parents make mistakes, they can partially recover by finding a silver lining in the situation and use it as a teaching moment. "Alexander, I didn't provide the after-school supervision you needed, and you got into trouble. Both of us now have a better understanding of what goes on in this neighborhood when I'm not here."

Parents need to remember that even if they do things right, children have a mind of their own and are capable of defying instruction and making poor choices. When that happens, parents are responsible only for how they respond to those choices and for evaluating what can be done differently in the future. Especially for older children, there is a limit to how much responsibility parents should absorb.

CONCLUSION

The parenting practices that keep children drug free are the same that turn out industrious, honest, and mature young men and women. Teens need a lot of supervision and guidance. They are on the threshold of the adult world without the know-how or wisdom to navigate it on their own. When parents let children vegetate in front of the television or give them substantial unsupervised time with peers, they create fertile soil for habits of self-indulgence.

For teens already practicing the drug habit, parents should avoid any rehab program that follows the disease model, which is almost every one of them. The rehab option will sound deceptively attractive, but it is expensive, it generates drama, and it does nothing to compel sobriety. Drug-savvy children respond to consequences, not words.

Another of my incarcerated patients had a cocaine habit that started when he was a teen. He graduated from several rehab programs, which he now says were little more than temporary rescue operations. He said what he needed then was not to be rescued but to be restrained.

Parents should aggressively restrain their children from street drugs and the drug subculture. They have to make drug use so uncomfortable that it becomes painful and make sobriety so attractive that it becomes compelling.

12

CONTROLLING
ADULT DRUG USE

One of the unintended consequences of the disease model is that substance abusers achieve fairly substantial habits before they come to the attention of the medical and legal professionals whose job it is to control drug use. Those who are closest to addicts—family members, friends, and coworkers—have been marginalized. Laypeople often spend years enabling addicts because they believe they are helping sick people. If laypeople are given any responsibility, it is to get addicts to their rehab appointments. "I'm not a doctor" is a sad but oft-heard response from parents and spouses.

Deprofessionalizing substance abuse allows laypeople to intervene much earlier. Once substance abuse is no longer viewed as an illness, laypeople will feel free—and indeed will feel some responsibility—to take action at the earliest signs of a problem.

If society quits enabling substance abuse, most addicts would likely transition to moderate levels of use on their own. There would simply be no more marginal benefit in heavy, unremitting use—no more forbidden fruit, no more victim status, and no more transfer payments. When society's expectations change—from "You're addicted; you can't stop" to "Stop the drama and grow up"—we will likely watch a vast sea change in the behavior of the addicted class.

Recall that habits are practiced as long as they bring comfort and are abandoned when they cause pain. The key to minimizing drug abuse is to make irresponsible consumption so painful that responsible use becomes the only viable option.

In what follows, I offer a number of suggestions for establishing both formal and informal cultural controls. While the latter will be the more effective, several statutory changes are necessary for informal controls to do their work.

LEGISLATIVE CHANGES

The most important statutory change, of course, is the repeal of drug prohibition. States should begin to approach drugs like they do alcohol and tobacco: by taxing and regulating them. State officials must be careful not to be too aggressive with taxation because they will create alternative markets. In New York City, for instance, a pack of cigarettes costs over $9. At a nearby Indian reservation, where tobacco is not taxed, cigarettes cost half as much. One reservation sells about $35 million worth of cigarettes each month, enough to keep all smokers in the city supplied with one pack per day for three and a half months. The state of New York consequently loses about $576 million in tax revenue each year.[1]

States should continue to impose—and in some cases stiffen—criminal penalties for drug or alcohol use that endangers public safety. Those charged with protecting the public (police officers, public transportation operators, and so on) should face criminal penalties for any use on the job. On public roadways, we should continue to prosecute drivers who operate under the influence of any drug that impairs judgment. And we should never refer violators of driving-under-the-influence (DUI) laws to addiction specialists. Mothers Against Drunk Driving (MADD) supports mandatory substance abuse evaluations for anyone arrested for a DUI,[2] and currently thirty-six states have such laws on the books. On the contrary, states should repeal these referral laws. Why send DUI offenders to disease model advocates who will teach that substance abusers cannot control themselves? MADD officials, an otherwise smart group of people who understand the power of sanctions, have been seduced by the false promises of the disease model.

Federal and state governments should immediately end all payments to addiction treatment programs and end all mandates that private insurance companies pay for treatment. The Patient Protection and Affordable Care Act (2010) will need to be amended to remove the requirement for drug rehab coverage. Automobile and life insurance companies should remain free to charge higher premiums for those who have substance-abusing habits.

Welfare subsidies of any kind are great enablers. Therefore, transfer payments should always be dependent on negative drug tests or on reduced benefits if recipients choose to use drugs or alcohol. The Americans with Disabilities Act will need to be amended to remove any protections for alcohol and drug misuse. Showing up drunk for work is currently protected if employees volunteer for rehab. Employers should develop clear guidelines that specify company policies regarding substance use and then follow through with established sanctions.

Substance use itself should never be a crime unless, of course, it affects the safety of others. Otherwise, substance use should be of no consequence to any criminal proceeding. Since substance use is not inconsistent with responsible behavior, it should never be invoked to either mitigate or enhance criminal culpability.

Government health officials might decide to support drug prevention programs, but their efforts should never resemble temperance-era or disease model–era scare tactics. Prevention efforts should be educational in nature, stressing the mental and physical consequences of drug and alcohol use and key features of the habit model and remind the citizenry that there are criminal sanctions for supplying drugs to minors and for any use that affects the safety of others.

Drug rehab programs based on the disease model would be free to operate, but only the very wealthy would be able to afford them. Traditional drug treatment would come to resemble Dr. Drew Pinsky's "Celebrity Rehab"—a spa-like atmosphere populated by drama-and-attention-seeking celebrities.

There would still be a market for drug and alcohol counselors, but I suspect that most of their clients would be family members requesting help with incentivizing addicts. Counselors would also have a useful role to play in teaching addicts about habits, neuroplasticity, and human resourcefulness.

THE INTRACTABLE SUBSTANCE ABUSER

In chapter 9, we discussed a class of substance abusers who do not seem to respond to normal incentives. They are chronically intoxicated and homeless and have nothing left to lose. Even with the new cultural controls I propose in this book, some will still end up this way.

Currently, homeless substance abusers hover in and around inner-city rescue missions where they are given regular meals and warm beds. During the day, they panhandle and engage in petty theft to support their habits. They commit numerous acts of indecency, such as urinating on sidewalks and napping in bus shelters or on park benches.

According to the habit model, charitable organizations like rescue missions are enabling substance abusers. They are rescuing the wrong people. If they want to help, they should support those who have been left destitute by substance-abusing spouses or parents.

If these organizations would shift their focus away from the substance abuser, homeless addicts would have no place to go, which is precisely where we want them. With no benefactors and no sources of economic support, society could then enforce antiloitering laws and civilly commit these individuals to what I will call community reemployment centers (CRCs). These would be detention facilities that serve as alternatives to jails for homeless individuals who are "down on their luck."

The purpose of the CRCs would be to instill a work ethic—and little else. There would be no moralizing about drugs or alcohol. The reason: consuming them is not inconsistent with a strong work ethic. Many drug and alcohol users currently support their families and meet other obligations of responsible citizenship. That is the behavior we want to reinforce.

Labor in the CRCs would be provided primarily by government agencies for work that typically involves outside contracts: street and park cleaning, custodial work, lawn mowing, snow shoveling, and so on. Private employers could also interview and hire detainees. CRC supervisors would keep detailed records on work performance, skills, and attitudes and make these available to prospective employers.

Living arrangements would be austere but would provide nutritional meals, warm beds, and the opportunities for educational classes in the evenings. Labor wages would be kept low—near minimum wage—and would be garnished in three important ways: 1) to reimburse the state for the costs of room and board; 2) to pay for any fines, restitution, or medical treatment that was incurred in the process of commitment; and 3) mandatory savings accounts that would be used to establish detainees in the community on completion of their commitments.

Magistrates would do best to set the terms of commitments to end when specified financial goals are met. For instance, a civil commitment could be set to end when a detainee saved enough for six months of room and board with a security deposit. The CRC would then transfer that amount to a landlord of the detainee's choice. Any leftover funds would be given to detainees, who might need to buy work uniforms and supplies for jobs acquired during their detentions.

Commitments that depend on meeting financial goals are preferable to time-based detentions. Many chronic addicts have already served time in prisons and jails. They know how to do time—they sleep through it. Setting financial goals would force them to be industrious.

Those who refuse to work would be kept in jail-like cells. They would be fed but would have no liberties until they decide to go back to work. Obviously, if detainees have to meet financial goals, they would make no progress by refusing to work. Criminal behavior in the CRCs would be handled like it is everywhere else in society: the police would be called, and arrested detainees would be transferred to local jails.

CRCs would benefit society in many ways: they would rid our inner cities of much of the loitering and indecent behavior that currently exists, they would empty the jails of nonviolent substance abusers, and they would instill a work ethic on those least likely to have one. The only other approach to this population is the laissez-faire option, which many would find unpalatable.

INFORMAL CULTURAL CONTROLS

Informal controls are the instinctive behaviors that responsible people use to guard themselves and their families from irresponsible behavior. They hold the most promise for keeping drug and alcohol use within acceptable limits. And they will work as long as social service organizations and government agencies do not enable irresponsible behavior. Unfortunately, this is precisely what happens today with the widespread panoply of welfare and social services available to substance abusers.

What follows is a list of suggested guidelines for the informal control of drug and alcohol use. It is not an exhaustive list, but it illustrates the principles of effective embedded controls. These suggestions require no guidance or training from professionals. Most of these controls are instinctive and automatic. They require only that responsible laypeople act in their own self-interest. Abstinence should not be the goal; self-control in all behavior should be the goal.

- Never view the controlled consumption of drugs, alcohol, or tobacco as threats to society or as a stain on one's moral fiber.
- Never blame drugs or alcohol for irresponsible behavior.
- Show people respect by holding them responsible for their own behavior.
- Be swift to condemn any behavior that adversely affects you or those you love.
- Never apologize for doing so.
- Ostracize irresponsible people from your social circles.
- Call the police if you know that someone is driving under the influence.
- Get to know the police officers who patrol your neighborhood; they are a wonderful resource when you need someone escorted off the premises.
- Never make yourself responsible for teaching other adults how to behave.
- Never make yourself responsible for the behavior of other adults.
- Let your house guests know what your rules are in regard to drugs, alcohol, and tobacco.
- If you allow drug and alcohol use in your home, make sure it comes after everyone has met their respective responsibilities.
- Never date a substance abuser.
- Never marry a substance abuser.
- If your spouse becomes a substance abuser, issue a clear ultimatum, then follow through with it.
- Never say to a substance abuser, "You need help."
- If a minor child is caught using drugs or alcohol, see chapter 11.
- Drug counselors are useful only to the extent that they help family members set consequences for substance abusers.
- Buy only health insurance policies that do not force you to subsidize the addiction treatment industry.
- Protect your financial assets from irresponsible people.
- Substance abusers frequently lie; always be skeptical of them.
- Never try to get the "truth" out of a substance abuser.
- Never bail substance abusers out of jail.

- Never make excuses for substance abusers.
- Never provide meals, housing, or money to substance abusers.
- Give aid to those who have been adversely affected by substance abusers.
- When former substance abusers have transformed their lives, welcome them back with open arms.
- If they return to their substance-abusing habits, send them away.

CONCLUSION

Informal cultural controls have the power to shape addictive behavior because everyone wants respect and everyone wants to experience physical comfort. When these are reserved for those who behave responsibly, then society unleashes powerful forces that promote civil behavior—not just with drug consumption but with almost all human behavior.

13

CHALLENGES AND OPPORTUNITIES

Rejecting the disease model and legalizing drugs will be discomforting for many reasonable people. Medical science, after all, has enhanced our lives in so many important ways, and the disease approach has solid support within the scientific community. Many thoughtful people will also oppose legalizing drugs because of concerns that it will lead to runaway drug use. Others will wonder whether we can successfully navigate drug prohibition for children when drugs are legal for adults. And what about "by prescription only?" What role will the medical profession play if it loses its legal monopoly on the control of habit-forming drugs?

These are all valid issues, and I address each below. I also argue that the habit model presents new possibilities for understanding other deviant behaviors and in offering potentially more effective interventions. The disease model has expanded to "explain" many other compulsive behaviors. I think the neuroscientific record will show, however, that the habit model is a better fit for most, if not all, of these behaviors.

LEGALIZATION AND DRUG CONSUMPTION

It is probably true that average per capita consumption of habit-forming drugs will increase after drug legalization, but this does not necessarily translate into more problems. After the repeal of alcohol prohibition, alcohol consumption rose, but there were fewer social problems because society became less violent and more stable and beverage alcohol was safer to consume.[1] During prohibition, beverage alcohol was often adulterated with dangerous compounds.

Habit-forming drugs would also become less potent, or at least not continue to rise in potency. Prohibition creates economic and environmental forces that lead to more concentrated forms of drugs. This is known as the "Iron Law of Prohibition,"[2] and it led to an increase in hard liquor consumption (at the expense of beer and wine) during alcohol prohibition and to the emergence of crack cocaine and methamphetamine—both concentrated forms of their parent compounds—during drug prohibition. Legalization would also allow users to spread out their consumption rather than force it into small time slots, which is necessary under prohibition to compensate for later periods when clandestine opportunities might not be available.

The power of expectations also plays an important role. Drug legalization would impose a set of expectations that fosters moderation: drugs can be used responsibly, they do not overtake human behavior, and users are expected to conduct themselves civilly. Nothing about prohibition fosters moderation.

Ethan Nadelmann of the Drug Policy Alliance Network has made the point that in 1933, most people were old enough to remember what life had been like when alcohol was legal.[3] They knew that most of the noise about "demon rum" came from overzealous temperance supporters and not from real problems with alcohol. Voters recognized that prohibition was an experiment that went awry and were thus willing to reverse it after seeing its unintended consequences.

Today, on the other hand, no one is old enough to remember what life was like when cocaine, heroin, and marijuana were legal. The Harrison Act of 1914 initiated important social changes that continue to this day. No one is alive who can report that drugs were not significant social problems when they were legal or that most of the noise about drugs was coming from people with political agendas.

Fears about legalization also need to be juxtaposed with the real and present dangers of prohibition. At times when you have been waiting in the checkout line of the grocery store, the man behind you has been slamming methamphetamine for three days and now needs something for his stomach. He is paranoid and is trying to maintain his composure in public. His whole life is clandestine and crime laden, and he gets anxious because the authorities really are after him. He looks at you and ponders if you are in on it too. He watches when you scratch your chin and wonders if this is your signal to the cameras that one of "them" is behind you. He engages his logic—what is left of it—and tries to convince himself that your gesture is a mere coincidence. This is a good thing because he has a Glock .38 tucked into his waistband. He does not want to create a scene, but he is not going to be cornered. It is a highly charged, precarious moment as you casually peruse the cover of a tabloid.

Under a new social compact of drug legalization, with its new set of expectations, if the man behind you has been consuming meth, he has probably not been consuming as much, and he is likely to be armed with nothing more than a quip about the magazine you are reading. You will walk away with the impression that he seemed rather talkative.

PROHIBITION FOR CHILDREN WHEN DRUGS ARE LEGAL FOR ADULTS

To control drug use in children, we would use the model we now use with alcohol: establish a minimum age for purchasing and consuming drugs and ensure that there are penalties for supplying drugs to children. Some will say, however, that this is not working very well. In 2010, the percentages of eighth, tenth, and twelfth graders who admitted drinking an alcoholic beverage in the month prior to the survey were 14, 29, and 41 percent, respectively.[4] On the other hand, binge drinking among these age-groups has declined significantly since the peaks reached in the early 1990s. Proportional decreases from 1992 to 2010 have been 46, 32, and 26 percent, respectively.

Part of the ongoing problem with alcohol use among children might be due to the way we have subsumed alcohol abuse under the disease model. Even the popular Drug Abuse Resistance Education (D.A.R.E.) program, which teaches useful skills to children, nevertheless supports the disease model and recommends rehab for children who become "addicted" to alcohol.

As discussed in chapter 11, parents sometimes become passive participants in alcohol prevention efforts. They imagine that preventing drug and alcohol abuse is a job for the experts. I have known parents who have hauled their high school children into mental health clinics just to have them checked for addictions after their kids have come home drunk for the first time. By now, most should be aware of where those efforts lead.

One of the more interesting trends being used to control alcohol abuse on college campuses is based on "social norms theory." Developed at Hobart and William Smith colleges, this effort recognizes that a lot of dangerous behavior is influenced by faulty assessments of what is normal. Children and young adults often engage in unhealthy, risky behavior because they believe everyone else is doing it. The truth is that people tend to be more restrained than is commonly perceived. The loudest, most out-of-control behavior tends to get the most attention, and so it skews perceptions of what is normal. When young adults are given accurate information about the behaviors and perceptions of their peers, they tend to be less likely to engage in such patterns themselves.[5] The research shows that these efforts lead to less binge drinking and fewer legal consequences connected to alcohol abuse on campus. Social norms theory shows, again, the power of expectations.

Sadly, drug and alcohol addictions tend to consistently land in the top five fears that parents have regarding their children.[6] I think we do a disservice to children by adopting such fears because we paradoxically enhance the "forbidden-fruit" effect. Given the natural predilection that children have to be antagonistic toward their parents' beliefs, we should tell children that they are not allowed to use drugs and alcohol not because they can get addicted but because children are not mature enough to handle them. This is the most honest and realistic response, and it might lead some children to begin acting more maturely—just to prove their parents wrong.

Another method to combat the forbidden-fruit effect is a point made in chapter 11: allowing parents to closely supervise occasional drug or alcohol use in the home for any substances commonly used by the parents. State laws could allow for this exception. It would be best to have such practices anchored to cultural events such as religious or holiday celebrations. The one thing to avoid, though, is allowing groups of children to clandestinely consume on their own.

BY PRESCRIPTION ONLY

The medical profession's control of habit-forming drugs is a relatively recent phenomenon, dating only to 1914 for opium and cocaine, to

1937 for marijuana, and to the period from 1938 to 1951 for every other drug. The only drugs exempted from this control, of course, have been alcohol (since 1933) and nicotine, which are as habit forming as any other substance. During alcohol prohibition, doctors were the only legal sources of alcohol, as it required only a prescription. During the 1920s, the number of Walgreens stores increased from 20 to 400 as the demand was high for "medicinal" whiskey.[7]

Drug legalization, or self-medication as it is sometimes called, would be a big change for the medical profession. If people wanted Valium (diazepam), Dexedrine (amphetamine), or marijuana, most would buy directly from a licensed pharmacy or drug outlet and bypass their physician's office altogether. Doctors would not lose their status as medication experts, however, and many people would still seek their opinions and prescriptions as they did prior to 1938, when 25 percent of pharmacy drug sales were still by physician prescription.[8]

People with chronic illnesses such as back pain, HIV, or chronic fatigue could then buy all the opiates, marijuana, or amphetamines they need and would no longer have to do battle with their doctors; there would be no more manipulation, feigning, or embellishing. While physicians have been more liberal with pain prescriptions in recent years, many patients with severe, chronic pain are still undermedicated. If people could prescribe their own medications, they would be free to use as much as they thought they needed, and if they exceeded their doctors' recommendations, they would have no one to blame but themselves when there are complications. When self-medication fails to deliver—as it so often does—patients will be more receptive when they go back to their physicians to learn about other options. The notion that consumers should have access to whatever drugs they desire will become more palatable after reviewing the history of "by prescription only" and how that is currently working.

In 1938, Congress passed—and President Roosevelt signed—the Food, Drug, and Cosmetic Act. This required the Food and Drug Administration (FDA) to certify that all drugs on the market were safe for their recommended uses and dosages. This legislation came on the heels of the sulfanilamide disaster of 1937. The S. E. Massengill drug company wanted to market a liquid form of its popular antibiotic. The company chemists found that sulfanilamide dissolved readily in diethylene glycol, which turned out to be toxic to humans but now has many uses in solvents, lubricants, and antifreeze. They marketed it as "Elixir Sulfanilamide," and 107 people died shortly after consuming it.

The FDA prosecuted Massengill under the Pure Food and Drug Act (1906) for mislabeling the drug. "Elixir" is a term reserved for drugs dissolved in alcohol, not antifreeze. Until 1938, manufacturers were required only to accurately list the contents of their medicines; safety was "regulated" by liability lawsuits in the free market, and Massengill paid monetary settlements to the families of the deceased.[9]

Prior to 1938, the FDA controlled only product labeling require ments, and this created ongoing clashes with drug companies. The FDA wanted increasing amounts of information on labels—indications, doses, potential side effects, and so on—all with the goal of increasing the public's knowledge to make self-medication safe. One drug company executive complained, however, that they were being forced to provide "a correspondence course in medicine" to laypeople.[10]

Congress listened to these concerns and created an exemption in the 1938 act. If manufacturers placed a label that read, "Caution: To be used only by or on the prescription of a physician," companies would be exempted from having to provide any further information. In fact, if companies wanted to include any other labeling information for prescription-only drugs, the FDA required that the warnings be so esoteric that they were unintelligible to laypeople.[11]

This exemption diminished the liability that drug companies faced and transferred that risk to doctors, who, not surprisingly, were willing to assume it. But which drugs would be labeled "by prescription only" was left up to the drug companies, and this soon created problems for FDA officials. Some packages were marketed as prescription only, and other packages of the same drug had full prescribing information and were marketed directly to consumers. Companies realized that statements like "by prescription only" or "for physician use only" increased the appeal of these drugs; they gave the impression that these were particularly potent medications. Such drugs sold briskly when marketed directly to consumers. Retail pharmacies were just as willing to disregard packaging requirements and often sold prescription-only drugs over the counter.

FDA officials increasingly sought to remove from drug companies the authority to decide which drugs were to be prescription-only, and officials were partially successful when Congress passed the 1951 Durham-Humphrey Amendment to the Food, Drug, and Cosmetic Act.

(Both Representative Carl Durham and Senator Hubert H. Humphrey were pharmacists before entering Congress). The bill specified that if a drug was habit forming or had potentially harmful effects when used by a layperson, then its status by law was to be prescription-only.

Another pharmaceutical tragedy in 1961 was used to expand the FDA's authority: the thalidomide disaster. Thalidomide was marketed worldwide as a sedative in the late 1950s. A New Drug Application to sell it in the United States was submitted in 1960. The FDA's Dr. Frances Kelsey delayed approval of the drug so that she could investigate reports that the drug caused neurological problems.[12] While the application was still pending, reports surfaced that thalidomide was causing severe congenital abnormalities in the forty-seven countries in which it had been sold. "Thalidomide babies" had truncated limbs—stumps for arms and legs. A few babies in the United States were affected from thalidomide obtained abroad.

The thalidomide experience was the pretext for the 1962 Kefauver-Harris Amendments, which gave vast new powers to the FDA. All drug companies now had to submit data showing safety in pregnancy, and the FDA was to approve all human trials, drug advertising, labeling, and manufacturing. The law gave the agency exclusive authority to determine which drugs could be sold over the counter and required drug companies to prove that their new drugs were "effective" for their indicated purposes. This was intended to keep drugs off the market that were ineffective yet popular because of the charisma and "testimonials" of those marketing the drugs.[13]

There are four historical caveats about the "by prescription only" story that shed light on drug legalization. First, the prescription-only label never arose from problems related to self-medication. Prescription-only was an industry-supported effort designed to shift the liability risk from manufacturers to the medical profession. The head of the FDA in fact testified in Senate hearings that nothing in the proposed legislation of 1938 was designed to prevent or inhibit self-medication.[14]

Second, neither the sulfanilamide nor the thalidomide disaster makes a case for the prescription-only designation. Almost all the casualties in these episodes came from physician prescriptions.[15] The lesson to draw is that there is wisdom in taking time to ensure that drugs are safe or at least in knowing the risks before drugs come on the market. Thalidomide, by the way, has been back on the market since 1998 and is used in the treatment of certain hematologic cancers and as an immune-boosting agent with strict warnings and controls designed to keep it away from pregnant women.

Third, after 1938 there was little or no opposition to how the FDA's incremental increase in powers supplanted individual rights to self-medicate. A House minority report made note of this encroachment on individual liberty prior to the 1951 legislation but nevertheless supported shifting control to the FDA. Any opposition came from drug manufacturers, and it was about their own rights to choose which products would be prescription-only. Drug manufacturers claimed that the FDA and the Truman administration were instituting "socialized medicine" by making decisions that the free market had traditionally made.

Finally, the loss of individual self-medication rights occurred at the same time that the disease model was gaining steam and reflected the growing sentiments among the scientific and political elite that laypeople were not capable of making safe choices for themselves. Preserving individual freedoms was still important in the 1938 legislation, but between then and the 1960s, the shift to "protection by experts" became complete.

Returning to the pre-1938 freedom to self-medicate is arguably safer today because of the many sources of rapid, Internet-based drug education available to consumers. Any attempt, though, to outlaw "for prescription only" will be opposed by almost all medical doctors and FDA officials who are highly invested in maintaining their present positions of influence. They will recite stories of how some people self-medicate in harmful ways. Not mentioned will be the fact that self-medication is already a thriving practice today.

For instance, the entire prescription drug market (habit forming and otherwise) in the United States in 2008 was estimated at $234 billion.[16] The annual U.S. illicit cannabis market alone has been conservatively estimated at anywhere from $15 billion to $40 billion, and some estimates put it much higher.[17] For heroin the figure is $8 billion, and for cocaine the value is $37 billion.[18] These three street drugs alone conservatively account for one-third the size of the legal prescription market for all drugs.

When we add in the alcohol-beverage market, which has been estimated at $188 billion, and tobacco products at $90 billion, the current market of self-medication with habit-forming drugs in the United States is already larger than the entire prescription-only drug market.

There is virtually no chance of alcohol ever again becoming "by prescription only," but recent legislation moves tobacco products a step in that direction. In June 2009, President Obama signed the Family Smoking Prevention and Tobacco Control Act, which gives broad new powers to the FDA to regulate the marketing and content of tobacco products. The law specifically prohibits the FDA from outlawing nicotine, but it has the option to regulate the nicotine content of tobacco products.

This presents a dilemma for regulators. If they lower nicotine content, people might smoke more to reach their accustomed level, which would then increase their exposure to the many other toxins in hot cigarette smoke. If they lower nicotine too much, a black market might appear, and states would lose a large tax opportunity while inciting crime and violence.

Fortunately, Congress was aware of these unintended consequences and rightfully limited the power of the FDA—or maybe they were influenced by the powerful tobacco lobby. Regardless, tobacco products are freely available to those who want them, and society experiences zero violence related to the tobacco trade. The fact that smoking can lead to lung cancer and other ailments is not a reason to ban tobacco, but it might be a reason to make smokers pay a greater share of their health care costs.

If habit-forming drugs were legally sold at licensed pharmacies or dispensaries, proprietors should be free to refuse to sell to certain individuals but should never be held responsible for anyone's use of the substances they sell. For instance, pharmacists may refuse to sell amphetamines to underweight customers or refuse to sell Valium to people who appear intoxicated. For drugs that have special safety concerns, we can still keep strict safety controls. For instance, there are ways to keep thalidomide out of the hands of women of childbearing age and still have it be legal, as it is today.

THE HABIT MODEL AND OTHER DEVIANT BEHAVIORS

There are other behaviors that share important features with drug and alcohol abuse: excessive gambling, sex, overeating, and chronic criminality, to name a few. They all include complex rituals, psychological rewards, cue-induced arousal, withdrawal symptoms, and impaired decision making.

Brain imaging studies have shown that obese rats[19] and human pathological gamblers[20] have deficits in neural reward pathways and heightened cue-induced craving. These are findings similar to those seen in substance abusers. The disease model posits that changes like these cause people to reach a point where they are unable to learn from their risky behaviors. They fail to experience the rewards that nonaddicted people experience, and thus they compulsively engage in risky behaviors in vain attempts to achieve pleasure.

Every criticism of the disease model of substance abuse can be applied to disease models that are used to explain other deviant or compulsive behaviors. When brain scientists find deficits in neural reward pathways, for example, it is appropriate to question whether they are observing 1) disease states, 2) the biological correlates of character traits, or 3) the normal neuroplastic changes that occur in response to repetitive behaviors.

The answer, of course, depends on how one defines a disease and how one chooses to view human nature. What should be clear, however, is that empirical science does not provide much guidance. This is a philosophical issue; how people resolve it drives how they then view the science that is before them.

Regardless of one's devotion to disease models, it is important to note how they play out in the real world. Let me illustrate with one example: how the scientific community attempts to explain chronic criminal behavior. An important study recently found that a group of twenty-three-year-old criminals in Mauritius had significantly reduced fear-conditioning skin responses at three years of age compared to a matched group of three-year-olds who did not become criminals twenty years later.[21] Skin responses are a good measure of psychological stress, and this study showed that as early as three years of age, those who show little fear in life are, as a group, at risk of becoming criminals as adults. An important note is that the study found a group difference only. There is no indication that any individual skin response is predictive of criminality since diminished skin responses will be found among noncriminals and many normal skin responses will be found among criminals. Elissa P. Benedek, a past president of the American Psychiatric Association, opined that the skin-response research shows that "early brain dysfunction" can lead to criminal behavior.[22]

Did this research identify "brain dysfunction," or did it identify a character trait? The case can be made that this study identified a biological correlate of only part of what it takes to become a criminal—lack of fear. Most of the criminals I have worked with readily admit that they have little fear of others or of getting into trouble with the law. Yet these fearless individuals are perfectly able to adjust their behavior whenever it suits their needs. For instance, when they want to get out of prison on time, they will refrain from fighting (a common habit in prisons) in order to avoid losing "good" time. I have also seen these fearless individuals work hard to avoid violating even minor prison rules so they do not lose the privilege of playing with their teams in prison-based softball leagues.

When the medical profession views prosocial behavior as arising from healthy brains and criminal behavior as arising from disordered brains, it fails to appreciate the opportunism of human nature and derails a host of effective cultural controls. Those who lack fear will avoid criminal behavior when the disincentives are sufficiently strong. Lay society is well positioned to establish meaningful disincentives, but when laypeople hear that "disordered brains" cause criminal behavior, they back off, and instead yield to a criminal justice system that has abandoned most notions of punishment in favor of therapy.

The loss of effective cultural controls over deviant behavior starts early in life and is due in large part to the very book that informs the disease model: the psychiatric profession's *Diagnostic and Statistical Manual of Mental Disorders* (*DSM*).

First printed in 1952, the *DSM* had humble beginnings. It was created to organize and classify the emotional and behavioral struggles that people experience. This was important because the mental health field was in need of standardization. Different clinicians were giving different labels to similar presentations, and, conversely, people with completely different presentations were being given similar labels. There was no recognized authority to govern consistency.

Now in its fourth edition and listing over 400 labels, the *DSM* had the predicted effect of getting all clinicians on the same sheet of music. And being a classification manual, it has a label for just about every imaginable presentation.

In the 1960s and 1970s, the manual began to take on a life of its own. Policymakers at the federal and state levels started requiring health insurance companies to reimburse doctors and hospitals for using the *DSM*. This was at the height of the deinstitutionalization movement, and officials wanted to ensure that the mentally ill were receiving treatment in the community. All of a sudden, those classification labels were reified into bona fide medical illnesses. What originally had been a classification manual quickly became a diagnostic manual.

Because no brain abnormalities or "chemical imbalances" are known to exist[23] for behavior problems (except in cases of dementia and traumatic brain damage), there is an intellectual sleight of hand at work. It is one thing to put labels on clusters of behaviors but quite another to claim that these labels represent brain disorders causing the behaviors in question.

How this works in the real world is as follows: a restless and fearless child who begins violating classroom rules (getting up out of his seat, talking out of turn, or bullying others), will be sent to a mental health clinic where he will be diagnosed with attention-deficit/hyperactivity disorder. When he begins fighting and setting fires, he will be diagnosed with conduct disorder. When he starts using drugs, he will be diagnosed with substance abuse disorder. When he begins to have volatile adolescent emotions, he will be diagnosed with bipolar affective disorder. Along the way, he will be sent to psychiatrists for medications, rehab for drug problems, and therapists for talk therapy.

The fact that psychiatric diagnoses are essentially labels does not imply that mental illness is not real, nor does it make light of the fact that there is a lot of emotional suffering in the world. It only means that label-making gets no one closer to understanding behavior problems or in knowing what to do about them. While the *DSM* no doubt captures the truly mentally ill, the book is so expansive that its reach is limited only by the ideological (or financial) interests of the diagnostician.

Labels probably help professionals more than anyone else; we in the field know the criteria sets, and when we say to a colleague that someone has "borderline personality disorder" or "intermittent explosive disorder," we know what each other is talking about. But while labels help us, they often have a negative impact on the parents, extended family members, and authorities who have to deal with unruly behavior in the community. Laypeople believe what they have been told by the experts: psychiatric diagnoses are brain disorders, and the brain controls behavior. Laypeople then defer to the experts, withholding what might be natural impulses to discipline a child in order not to compromise any therapeutic work. When police arrest lawbreaking teens who they know to be on medications, they often do the same thing. I have seen kids dropped off at clinics rather than being booked into juvenile detention.

It should not be a stretch to imagine how children raised in this kind of pharmacotherapeutic climate might develop emotional and behavioral habits that keep them from becoming self-controlled, responsible adults. Instead, they often become narcissistic, labile, and entitled adults. I have seen many older teens and young adults with chronic criminal behavior who I do not think have ever experienced anything that felt like punishment for their misdeeds. Each foray through the criminal justice system brings more labels, more services, and more hand-wringing from those in charge.

The next time Human Rights Watch reports that we have quadrupled the number of mentally ill prison inmates[24] or that the U.S. Justice Department reports that half of all inmates in jails and prisons are mentally ill,[25] readers will have a better idea of who is being counted as mentally ill and why so many of these people have criminal habits. Expanding traditional mental health services will not reduce these numbers. We will reduce them when we consistently reward good behavior and consistently punish bad behavior. For people who show little fear in life and who have no qualms about violating the rights of others, we might have to raise the bar—they might need stronger disincentives than other people—but there is no other way to nurture habits of socially appropriate behavior.

14

CONCLUSION

The disease model of substance abuse informs both fronts in the war on drugs: rehab for drug users and prohibition laws for drugs. The model arose from a political philosophy that views people as being controlled by their biological natures. Legitimate science never informed this view, but broad appeals to science and health have disguised the fact that the drug war is and always has been an ideological movement.

The modern disease model was the brainchild of early influential members of Alcoholics Anonymous, but it was adopted by progressive-minded politicians who wanted to show that they were using "science" to tackle ongoing anxieties about alcohol after the repeal of prohibition. Drug prohibitionists co-opted the disease model when racist and anti-immigrant sentiments were no longer in vogue. They were helped by the UN Single Convention's concerns for the "health and welfare of mankind."[1]

This is why those who favor a "harm reduction" approach to the drug war—legalizing drugs and shifting resources into more rehab—will never win the argument. Prohibition will always have a cloak of respectability as long as drug users are deemed to be "sick."

The medical profession, for its part, was not about to demur when federal and state governments enshrined rehab as official public policy. Medical science was forced to develop Ptolemic-like contortions to justify the new treatment, but none of them hold up well under close scrutiny.

The disease model thrives because it has many stakeholders: enlightened politicians, medical scientists, law enforcement officials, and addicts themselves. The model's psychological appeal is easy to understand: it is designed to help people, it appears to explain the inexplicable, and it falls well within the twentieth century's zeitgeist of having faith in the scientific community.

And therein lies the problem. Having experienced power abuses by clerical leaders throughout history, one would have thought that westerners would have had some degree of skepticism about men and women of science. But I think the science was too alluring. People saw the objectivity of the scientific method and assumed the same was true of scientists. It is true that the scientific method can uncover fascinating facts about the world around us, but one should never forget that human beings produce the stories that try to manage those facts.

While human nature has been written out of the substance abuse conversation, it sits everywhere like the elephant in the room. "Out-of-control" addicts are living off of sick-role benefits, cartels and organized gangs have so much wealth and power that they control the police in many areas of the world, the medical profession continues to trumpet the success of rehab, and when public officials are not taking bribes, they are draining billions of dollars from taxpayers to bolster their image as guardians of the world's health.

The zeal needed to fight the drug war can affect one's sense of balance and focus. The United Nations recently felt the need to caution leaders that "there is growing recognition that we must draw a line between *criminals* (drug traffickers) and their *victims* (drug users)."[2] The general lawlessness that drug prohibition creates is looked on as all the more reason to double-down.

Rethinking the drug war, then, involves important debates about the value of individual liberties and responsibilities, the role of government, and the proper place of science in society. Given the foregoing discussion, the only way to reasonably manage the drug problem is to embrace human nature in all its beauty and sordidness. There is no reason to view addicts as if they cannot control themselves or to treat traffickers as criminals or to view our leaders as exceptionally wise and in touch with science. Human nature is opportunistic, and we should respond in kind.

If we let people consume what they want but face the consequences of their own behavior, if we let traffickers sell what they want but we collect taxes on what they earn, and if we unseat leaders who develop messianic dispositions, then we will create a safer world for all of us and in the process validate another side of human nature: its tremendous resourcefulness.

APPENDIX A: SIGNS OF DRUG USE IN CHILDREN

Keeping kids drug free would be easier if there were clear and unmistakable signs. Unfortunately, this is not often the case. Sure, we might be able to smell alcohol on a child's breath or detect marijuana smoke on her clothing, but drug-using children are pretty good at hiding what they do, and many drugs do not leave traces. Some kids will also make a concerted effort to be more respectful and helpful at home for the very reason that they do not want to set off warning bells.

Detection is also complicated by the fact that the signs of drug use are often the same signs of normal adolescence: moodiness, irritability, arguing, slacking, anger, appetite changes, withdrawal from family, bad grades, and excessive sleeping. Parents have to make sure they do not assume that such behavior is indicative of drug use or that happy, compliant behavior is a sign of no drug use.

What follows is a list of drugs of abuse and several signs that all parents should know.

MARIJUANA

The smell of marijuana is easily detected by those who are familiar with it. It has a sweet, musty aroma and can usually be detected on clothing. Marijuana can also cause bloodshot eyes and the "munchies." Excessive and inappropriate laughter is also common.

SEDATIVE-HYPNOTICS

These drugs include barbiturates (phenobarbital and Seconal) and benzodiazepines (Valium, Ativan, Klonopin, and Xanax). These drugs mimic the signs of alcohol: unsteady gait, clumsiness, slurred speech, and inappropriate comments.

COCAINE

This drug can be snorted, smoked, or injected. Cocaine powder is snorted, usually through tightly wound dollar bills or straws. Crack cocaine, which is more highly concentrated, is smoked. Cocaine usually makes the user feel euphoric and energetic and leads to increases in body temperature, blood pressure, and heart rate. Seizures, abdominal pain, and nausea can result. The appetite is usually suppressed; regular users often lose weight. This has been a common weight-loss agent over the years, especially for women.

METHAMPHETAMINE

This is a very habit-forming stimulant that is a concentrated form of amphetamine. It causes intense, energetic highs that increase the heart rate and blood pressure. It is a white, odorless, bitter-tasting powder that is snorted or injected. It has a rocklike version called "crystal meth," which is heated and smoked. Like cocaine, this will also cause extreme weight loss and insomnia. Users can stay up for days on end and then sleep for days when they come off the drug. Meth use can also lead to profound behavioral changes that include paranoia, restlessness ("tweaking"), and abrupt acts of violence.

ECSTASY (MDMA)

This is a tablet or capsule that causes feelings of mental stimulation, emotional warmth, enhanced sensory perception, and increased energy. Adverse health effects can include nausea, chills, sweating, teeth clenching, muscle cramping, and blurred vision. MDMA can interfere with the body's ability to regulate temperature, which can occasionally be fatal if the body overheats. This drug is commonly used at "rave" parties and at nightclubs.

LSD (ACID)

LSD produces unpredictable psychological "trips" that produce delusions and hallucinations and last about twelve hours. The effects can be frightening and often lead to panic attacks. Physical effects include increased body temperature, heart rate, and blood pressure. Insomnia and loss of appetite are common. LSD is sold as tablets, capsules, or liquid or on absorbent small squares of paper called "stamps."

HEROIN

Heroin is a strong morphine-based drug that is usually injected, though it can be snorted or smoked. Intravenous heroin addicts are called "junkies." Heroin is a strong narcotic pain reliever. Short-term effects include euphoria and clouded thinking followed by alternating wakeful and drowsy states. Users typically "crash," which means they lie around for hours in a somnolent state—think of the nineteenth-century opium dens depicted in movies. In overdose, heroin depresses breathing, which is how heroin junkies often die. Users who inject the drug are at risk for infectious diseases such as HIV/AIDS and hepatitis.

PCP (PHENCYCLIDINE)

PCP is a synthetic drug sold as tablets, capsules, or a powder. It can be snorted, smoked, or eaten. It was developed in the 1950s as an anesthetic. Like ketamine discussed below, PCP causes "dissociation"—it distorts perceptions of sight and sound and produces feelings of detachment from the environment and self. At high doses it can cause unpredictable and violent behavior.

CLUB DRUGS

These are drugs commonly found in the nightclub scene. They include Ecstasy, methamphetamine, LSD, GHB, Rohypnol®, and ketamine. The first three are covered above. GHB and Rohypnol are brain depressants like the sedative-hypnotics. GHB was approved by the Food and Drug Administration in 2002 for use in the treatment of narcolepsy (a sleep disorder). GHB is usually ingested orally in either liquid or powdered form. Rohypnol (flunitrazepam) is a benzodiazepine like Valium. It has gained popularity in the United States since the early 1990s. Both of these drugs have a reputation as "date rape" drugs. They are odorless, colorless, and tasteless. They are usually sold in pill form and are frequently combined with alcohol and other beverages to incapacitate users.

Ketamine is an anesthetic used in veterinary practice. It causes "dissociation" similar to PCP. High doses can cause dreamlike states, hallucinations, delirium, and amnesia.

PRESCRIPTION DRUG ABUSE

Teen substance abusers often steal prescription drugs from family members, either for their own use or to sell for cash. Common prescription drugs that are abused or sold include narcotic pain pills (Oxycontin, Vicodin, Dilaudid, and Demerol), stimulants (Ritalin, Adderall, and Concerta), and benzodiazepines (Xanax, Valium, Ativan, and Klonopin).

Part of the reason we have seen an increase in teen prescription drug abuse is that doctors have been writing more prescriptions for these drugs. According to the National Institute on Drug Abuse, between 1991 and 2009, prescriptions for stimulants increased from 5 million to nearly 40 million, which is an eightfold increase. Prescriptions for narcotic analgesics increased from about 45 million to approximately 180 million, which is a fourfold increase.

INHALANTS

Inhalants are a diverse group of substances whose chemical vapors can be inhaled to produce mind-altering effects. A variety of common household products can be abused: spray paint, some glues, gasoline, paint thinner, and cleaning fluids. Young children and adolescents are familiar with this practice. If they have not "huffed" these substances themselves, they have heard about kids at school doing it.

The effects of inhalants are similar to those of alcohol and include slurred speech, lack of coordination, euphoria, and dizziness. Inhalants can also cause light-headedness, hallucinations, delusions, confusion, nausea, and vomiting.

By displacing air in the lungs, inhalants deprive the body of oxygen, which can damage cells throughout the body, but the cells of the brain are especially sensitive. Permanent memory problems or slowed thinking can result. High concentrations of inhalants can also cause death.

DRUG PARAPHERNALIA

These are items that are used to help transport or consume drugs. They include pipes, syringes, needles, and roach clips. The latter is for holding the burning end of a marijuana cigarette. Paraphernalia also includes razor blades, spoons, tightly rolled dollar bills, straws, empty pen casings, digital scales, vials, and small resealable plastic bags.

Lightbulbs are often used to smoke methamphetamine. The metal cap is removed, and meth is heated inside the bulb in order to vaporize it prior to smoking. I have talked to parents who began noticing that lightbulbs were missing from their home. This led to the discovery that their son was a meth addict. Other meth paraphernalia includes bottle caps and pieces of foil.

A NOTE ABOUT DRUG-TESTING

Home drug tests do not detect all the drugs listed above. There is no test, for instance, that identifies LSD, GHB, or inhalants. On the other hand, most teen drug users concurrently use marijuana and alcohol, which are readily detectable. By identifying these, parents will be able to identify most drug-using children.

APPENDIX B:
MEDICATIONS USED
TO TREAT ADDICTIONS

There are three types of medications that are approved by the Food and Drug Administration (FDA) for addictions: replacement therapies, anticraving medications, and blocking drugs. Their success has been much smaller than what would be predicted from the disease model and for one simple reason: addicts do not like taking them; they interfere with the experience of getting high. Below is a summary of each medication class.

REPLACEMENT MEDICATIONS

These are substitutes for drugs of abuse. They are similar in chemical composition but induce less intense highs and are prescribed under controlled supervision. Methadone and buprenorphine are FDA approved as heroin-replacement therapies. Since they do not provide as much of a "high," they are less likely to be abused or diverted to the black market. Buprenorphine is marketed as Subutex and Suboxone.

When methadone was first marketed in the 1960s, there was much hope that heroin addicts would become responsible members of society again. As one methadone treatment team recently reported, however, it is their impression that only 5 to 7 percent of methadone patients lead drug-free (other than methadone), productive lives.[1] Methadone is occasionally sold on the street, and surveys show that many methadone patients abuse other street drugs, as do up to 80 percent of patients taking buprenorphine. Of note is that methadone-related deaths lately have been skyrocketing. Between 1999 and 2005, deaths increased nearly fivefold to 4,462 per year, a number that researchers say is likely underestimated.[2] This sudden increase, though, appears to be the result of physicians increasingly prescribing it for pain control.

Nicotine replacement therapy comes in the form of chewing gum, skin patches, nasal spray, oral inhaler, and lozenges. These help lessen the intensity of withdrawal symptoms and also avoid the punishing effects of hot cigarette smoke on the respiratory system. While nicotine replacement therapy has helped some people, it has not significantly lessened the number of regular smokers. Smoked tobacco delivers faster and higher concentrations of nicotine, which are much more pleasurable than the muted effects of replacement preparations.

ANTICRAVING DRUGS

Craving is the subjective experience of desiring a drug. Craving is not just a psychological construct or idea. Its physiological correlates can be viewed on brain scans. For alcohol craving, the FDA has approved acamprosate (Campral). Its mechanism of action is unknown, but some people report less alcohol craving when taking it.

Some also report less craving with Naltrexone (Revia), which is an opiate receptor blocker. Part of the "high" from alcohol appears to be mediated by endogenous opiates. Theoretically, Revia should cut down on the pleasurable subjective experience of drinking alcohol, and some studies have shown a slight advantage over placebo.

Buproprion (Zyban) has been approved for nicotine craving. It is the antidepressant Wellbutrin. A number of other drugs have shown some success with cocaine craving: topiramate (Topamax), disulfiram (Antabuse), modafinil (Provigil), propranolol (Inderal), and baclofen (Lioresal).

Varenicline (Chantrix) is the newest anticraving drug, and it is designed for smoking cessation. In the brain, nicotine attaches to "nicotinic" receptors that are connected to the brain's reward system. Chantrix blocks these receptors so that smokers get less of a "high" and theoretically start to smoke less. The problem is that the drug appears to also block normal or nondrug feelings of pleasure. In early 2008, the FDA issued alerts about the high number of suicides occurring with

Chantrix. The Federal Aviation Administration has prohibited the use of the drug for pilots and air traffic controllers. The drug is expensive and has less than a 25 percent success rate at one year.

BLOCKING DRUGS

Medications that block euphoria are the most effective drugs in the world—and also the least effective. They work 100 percent of the time if you can get addicts to take them.

Naltrexone, for instance, completely blocks the effects of heroin and other opiates. But since most addicts enjoy opiate highs, they do not like to take naltrexone.

The other well-known blocking drug is disulfiram (Antabuse). Developed in the 1940s as a treatment for worm infestations, disulfiram impairs the metabolism of alcohol in the body. There are two steps in the breakdown of alcohol, and disulfiram inhibits the second step. This allows the by-product of the first step (acetaldehyde) to build up, which leads to a highly noxious experience. Elevated acetaldehyde causes nausea, vomiting, flushing, increased heart rate, and dizziness—in short, the kind of experience one wants to avoid at all costs.

Disulfiram takes seven to ten days to start working and the same amount of time to quit working. This helps avoid an impulsive return to drinking. One cannot decide in the morning to stop the pill and expect to go drinking that night. This lag can be helpful for individuals who feel they cannot control themselves and who want an additional external incentive.

APPENDIX C: DIAGNOSING ADDICTIONS

The area where one might expect neuroscience to play a prominent role is an area where it plays no role at all: making the diagnosis of an addiction. According to the *Diagnostic and Statistical Manual of Mental Disorders* (4th ed., text revision), there are two levels of drug addiction: "substance abuse" and "substance dependence."

The diagnosis of "substance abuse" is made when the following criterion is met:

1. The use of drugs or alcohol causes significant impairment in social, occupational, or educational endeavors, or it becomes dangerous or leads to legal problems.

The diagnosis of "substance dependence," which is the more severe of the two diagnoses, is made when one additional criterion is met:

2. There is evidence of withdrawal symptoms or tolerance, consumption is greater than intended, there are unsuccessful efforts to cut down, or one's life begins to center around consumption.

Looking closely, one will notice that these criteria are entirely subjective. For instance, who determines "significant impairment"? Even judgments regarding withdrawal and tolerance are made by simply asking addicts if they have had those experiences. Addicts often over-report their symptoms when seeking admission to rehab programs.

While it is safe to assume that people who come forward for help are experiencing significant problems, the "diagnosis" requires no special technical knowledge.

Doctors frequently order laboratory and radiological tests during substance abuse evaluations. Patients and their families often think these tests are necessary to establish the diagnosis. What clinicians are doing, however, is looking for damage to the body from drugs and alcohol. Physical damage, though, is not a criterion for the diagnosis.

In the end, the diagnosis is based on the subjective views of the diagnostician. In practice, diagnosticians are very liberal with these labels. While labels might help identify those who consume too much, labels get no one closer to understanding the problem or knowing how to deal with it.

NOTES

INTRODUCTION

1. American Psychiatric Association, American Psychiatric Association Position Statement on Substance Related Disorders, December 1995.

CHAPTER 1

1. Harry G. Levine, "The Discovery of Addiction: Changing Conceptions of Habitual Drunkenness in America," *Journal of Studies on Alcohol* 15 (1978): 493–506.

2. See chapter 7. Almost all addiction treatment programs today incorporate some aspect of the twelve-step model of Alcoholics Anonymous, which has close ties to traditional Protestant theology. Medical treatments that incorporate spiritual or theological principles appeal to the twin traditions of faith and reason that lie at the heart of Western society.

3. Benjamin Rush, *An Inquiry into the Effects of Ardent Spirits upon the Human Body and Mind* (Philadelphia: Bartam, 1805).

4. Interestingly, the same assumptions are active today. Despite huge advances in technology and in our ability to study the brain, no one part of the brain can be identified as the "will," and in almost all cases of deviant behavior, no brain pathology is known to exist.

5. Benjamin Rush, *Medical Inquiries and Observations on the Diseases of the Mind* (Philadelphia: B & T Kite, 1812), 264.

6. Sarah M. Tracy, *Alcoholism in America, from Reconstruction to Prohibition* (Baltimore, MD: Johns Hopkins University Press, 2007), 96.

7. Jim Baumohl and Robin Room, "Inebriety, Doctors, and the State: Alcoholism Treatment Institutions before 1940," in *Recent Developments in Alcoholism*, vol. 5, ed. Marc Galanter (New York: Plenum), 135–74.

8. Baumohl and Room, "Inebriety, Doctors, and the State."

9. Tracy, *Alcoholism in America, from Reconstruction to Prohibition*, 149.

10. Kathleen Thomsen Hall and Paul Appelbaum, "The Origins of Commitment for Substance Abuse in the United States," *Journal of the American Academy of Psychiatry Law* 30 (2002): 33–45.

11. Tracy, *Alcoholism in America, from Reconstruction to Prohibition*, 3.

12. Tracy, *Alcoholism in America, from Reconstruction to Prohibition*, xii.

13. James Parker, "Inebriate Asylums, and a Visit to One," *The Atlantic Monthly*, October 1868, 395.

14. Parker, "Inebriate Asylums, and a Visit to One," 398.

15. A letter written by Dr. T. D. Crothers was found in the papers of Dr. Turner, the first superintendent, after his death. It detailed widespread graft and corruption at the asylum. It can be viewed at http://nysasylum.com/doc1879c.htm (accessed July 18, 2011).

16. Baumohl and Room, "Inebriety, Doctors, and the State."

17. Tracy, *Alcoholism in America, from Reconstruction to Prohibition*, 147.

18. Tracy, *Alcoholism in America, from Reconstruction to Prohibition*, 187.

19. Tracy, *Alcoholism in America, from Reconstruction to Prohibition*, 85.

20. "Medicine: Keeley Cure." *Time Magazine*, September 24, 1939.

21. Tracy, *Alcoholism in America, from Reconstruction to Prohibition*, 117–18.

22. Elizabeth M. Armstrong, *Conceiving Risk, Bearing Responsibility: Fetal Alcohol Syndrome and the Diagnosis of Moral Disorder* (Baltimore, MD: Johns Hopkins University Press, 2003), 37.

23. Mariana Valverde, "Degeneration Theories," in *Alcohol and Temperance in Modern History; A Global Encyclopedia*, vol. 1, ed. Jack S. Blocker, David M. Fahey, and Ian R. Tyrrell (Santa Barbara, CA: ABC-CLIO, 2003), 189.

24. Baumohl and Room, "Inebriety, Doctors, and the State."

25. Armstrong, *Conceiving Risk, Bearing Responsibility*, 47.

26. Armstrong, *Conceiving Risk, Bearing Responsibility*, 47.

27. R. MacLeod, "The Edge of Hope: Social Policy and Chronic Alcoholism in England, 1870–1900," *Journal of the History of Medicine* 22 (1967): 215–45.

28. Harry S. Warner, Rev. Francis W. McPeek, and E. M. Jellinek, "Yale Summer School Lecturers, Alcohol, Science, and Society, Twenty-Nine Lectures with Discussions as Given at the Yale Summer School of Alcohol Studies," *Journal of Studies on Alcohol* 1945: 282.

CHAPTER 2

1. I Corinthians 6:19.

2. Lyman Beecher, *Six Sermons on the Nature, Occasions, Signs, Evils and Remedy of Intemperance* (Boston: T. R. Marvin, 1827), 38.

3. Peter Conrad and Joseph Schneider, *Deviance and Medicalization: From Badness to Sickness* (Philadelphia: Temple University Press, 1992), 84.

4. William B. Carpenter, *On the Use and Abuse of Alcoholic Liquors in Health and Disease* (Boston: Massachusetts Temperance Society, 1861), xviii.

5. Joseph R. Gusfield, "Moral Passage: The Symbolic Process in Public Designations of Deviance," *Social Problems* 15, no. 2 (1967): 183.

6. Harry G. Levine, "The Discovery of Addiction: Changing Conceptions of Habitual Drunkenness in America," *Journal of Studies on Alcohol* 39, no. 1 (1978): 143–74.

7. Norman H. Clark, *Deliver Us from Evil* (New York: Norton, 1976), 48.

8. Clark, *Deliver Us from Evil*, 132.

9. As quoted in Mark Thornton, "Alcohol Prohibition Was a Failure," CATO Policy Analysis No. 157, July 17, 1991.

10. Clark, *Deliver Us from Evil*, 150.

11. Edward Behr, *Prohibition: Thirteen Years That Changed America* (New York: Arcade Publishing, 1996), 103–4.

12. Clark, *Deliver Us from Evil*, 165.

13. Report on the Enforcement of the Prohibition Laws of the United States, National Commission on Law Observance and Enforcement (The Wickersham Commission Report on Alcohol Prohibition), January 7, 1931. See separate report by Henry W. Anderson at http://www.druglibrary.org/schaffer/library/studies/wick/anderson.htm.

14. Thornton, "Alcohol Prohibition Was a Failure."

15. Jackson Kuhl, "Book Review: Eight Million Sots in the Naked City: How Prohibition Was Imposed on, and Rejected by, New York," *Reason*, November 1, 2007.

16. John D. Rockefeller, "Letter to the Editor," *New York Times*, June 7, 1932.

17. Sarah M. Tracy, *Alcoholism in America: From Reconstruction to Prohibition* (Baltimore, MD: Johns Hopkins University Press, 2007), 21.

18. Joseph R. Gusfield, "Moral Passage: The Symbolic Process in Public Designations of Deviance," *Social Problems* 15, no. 2 (1967): 175.

CHAPTER 3

1. "Demon Exorcised," *Time*, March 14, 1938.

2. Harry S. Warner, Rev. Francis W. McPeek, and E. M. Jellinek, "Yale Summer School Lecturers, Alcohol, Science, and Society, Twenty-Nine Lectures

with Discussions as Given at the Yale Summer School of Alcohol Studies," *Journal of Studies on Alcohol* 1945: 463–64.

3. Alcoholics Anonymous, *Alcoholics Anonymous,* 4th ed. (New York: Alcoholics Anonymous, 2001), xxviii.

4. Ron Roizen, "The American Discovery of Alcoholism, 1933–1939," PhD diss., University of California, Berkeley, 1991.

5. "Scientists Launch Unbiased Study of Drink Problem; Form a Research Council to Amass Facts and Present Them for Discussion," *New York Times,* October 3, 1938, 1, 9.

6. Dwight Anderson, "Alcohol and Public Opinion," *Quarterly Journal of Studies on Alcohol* 3 (December 1942): 376–92.

7. C. Lester Walker, "What We Know about Drinking," *Harper's Magazine,* July 1950.

8. E. M. Jellinek, "Phases of Alcohol Addiction," *Quarterly Journal of Studies on Alcohol* 13 (1952): 673–84.

9. Robin Room, "Sociological Aspects of the Disease Concept of Alcoholism," *Research Advances in Alcohol and Drug Problems* 7 (1983): 56.

10. Robert Straus, "Problem Drinking in the Perspective of Social Change, 1940–1973," in *Alcohol and Alcohol Problems: New Thinking and New Directions,* ed. W. I. Filstead, J. I. Rossi, and M. Keller (Cambridge, MA: Ballinger, 1976), 47–48.

11. E. M. Jellinek, *The Disease Concept of Alcoholism* (New Haven, CT: College and University Press, 1960), 7–10.

12. Jellinek, *The Disease Concept of Alcoholism,* 69.

13. The story of Jellinek's academic credentials (or lack thereof) is well documented at http://www.roizen.com/ron/rr11.htm, accessed February 2, 2010.

14. Mark Keller, "The Origins of Modern Research and Responses Relevant to Problems of Alcohol: A Brief History of the First Center of Alcohol Studies," in *Research Advances in Alcohol and Drug Problems,* vol. 10, ed. L. T. Kozlowski et al. (New York: Plenum Press), 162–63.

15. Keller, "The Origins of Modern Research and Responses Relevant to Problems of Alcohol," 165.

16. Jellinek, *The Disease Concept of Alcoholism,* 12.

17. Ron Roizen, personal communication, July 24, 2011.

18. Sally Brown and David R. Brown, *Mrs. Marty Mann: The First Lady of Alcoholics Anonymous* (Center City, MN: Hazelden, 2001).

19. Members of the alcohol industry sat on the NCA board until 1979, when the federal government wanted all alcoholic beverages to include a label of health risks. The medical members of the board favored this move. Marty Mann felt that the NCA should not take a position, but members of the industry wanted a statement opposing the labeling requirement. They lost and eventually left the NCA's board.

20. S. J. Woolf, "The Sick Person We Call an Alcoholic." *New York Times Magazine*, April 21, 1946.

21. Ron Roizen, personal communication, July 22, 2011.

22. According to David and Sally Brown, this was one of more than fifty admissions for Smithers to hospitals for alcoholism treatment.

23. Brown and Brown, *Mrs. Marty Mann*, 233.

24. Thomas P. Pike, *Memoirs of Thomas P. Pike* (Pasadena, CA: Grant Dahlstrom at the Castle Press, 1979), 84.

25. Brenda Hewitt, *The History of NIAAA* (Bethesda, MD: National Institute on Alcohol Abuse and Alcoholism, 2006).

26. Pike, *Memoirs of Thomas P. Pike*, 251.

27. Roizen, "The American Discovery of Alcoholism, 1933–1939."

28. Ron Roizen, "Who Bought Whom? Revisiting 'Bowman's Compromise,'" June 10, 2011, http://pointsadhsblog.wordpress.com/2011/06/10/who-bought-whom-revisiting-%e2%80%9cbowman%e2%80%99s compromise%c2%80%9d/.

CHAPTER 4

1. James Samuelson, *The History of Drink: A Review, Social, Scientific, and Political* (London: Trubner & Co., 1878), 20.

2. Samuelson, *The History of Drink*, 20.

3. Carole L. Jurkiewicz and Murphy J. Painter, *Social and Economic Control of Alcohol: The 21st Amendment in the 21st Century* (Boca Raton, FL: CRC Press, 2008), 2.

4. 1 Timothy 4:4.

5. 1 Timothy 5:23.

6. 1 Corinthians 3:16–17, 5:11, 6:10; Galatians 5:19–21; Romans 13:3; Ephesians 5:18; Titus 2:3.

7. Samuelson, *The History of Drink*, 123.

8. G. Thomann, *Liquor Laws of the United States: Their Spirit and Effect*, 10th ed. (New York: U.S. Brewers Association, 1893), 132–33.

9. Paul L. Schiff Jr., "Opium and Its Alkaloids," *American Journal of Pharmaceutical Education* 66, no. 2 (Summer 2002): 186.

10. Schiff, "Opium and Its Alkaloids," 1.

11. Norman H. Clark, *Deliver Us from Evil: An Interpretation of American Prohibition* (New York: Norton, 1976), 218.

12. David F. Musto, *The American Disease: Origins of Narcotic Control*, 3rd ed. paperback (New York: Oxford University Press, 1999), 4.

13. Martin Booth, *Opium: A History* (London: Macmillan, 1999), 15.

14. Clark, *Deliver Us from Evil*, 220.

15. Musto, *The American Disease*, 28–36.

16. Musto, *The American Disease*, 71.

17. Musto, *The American Disease*, 7.

18. Text of the Harrison Narcotics Act (1914), Public Law No. 223, 63rd Cong., approved December 17, 1914.

19. See *Webb v. United States*, 249 U.S. 96 (1919), and *Jin Fuey Moy v. United States*, 254 U.S. 189 (1920).

20. Musto, *The American Disease*, 204.

21. Mark Thornton, "Alcohol Prohibition Was a Failure," CATO Policy Analysis No. 157, July 17, 1991.

22. Ross Coomber, *The Control of Drugs and Drug Users: Reason or Reaction?* (Amsterdam: Harwood Academic Publishers, 1998), 22.

23. Alexander Cockburn and Jeffrey St. Clair, *Whiteout: The CIA, Drugs, and the Press* (London: Verso, 1998), 72.

24. Rudolph J. Gerber, *Legalizing Marijuana: Drug Policy Reform and Prohibition Politics* (Westport, CT: Praeger, 2004), 9.

25. Richard J. Bonnie and Charles H. Whitebread, "The Forbidden Fruit and the Tree of Knowledge: An Inquiry into the Legal History of American Marijuana Prohibition," *Virginia Law Review* 56, no. 971 (October 1970): 1039.

26. Musto, *The American Disease*, 225.

27. Text of the Marihuana Tax Act of 1937.

28. United Nations, "Single Convention on Narcotic Drugs," http://www.unodc.org/pdf/convention_1961_en.pdf, 1961, 1.

29. Article 36, 1a.

30. Article 36, 1b.

31. National Commission, *The Report of the National Commission on Marijuana and Drug Abuse; Marijuana: A Signal of Misunderstanding, Commissioned by President Richard M. Nixon* (Washington, DC: National Commission, 1972).

32. Gene Weingarten, "Just What Was He Smoking," *Washington Post*, March 21, 2002.

33. *Dr. Marcus Conant, et al., Plaintiffs, v. Barry R. McCaffrey, et al., Defendants*, No. C 97-00139 WHA United States District Court for the Northern District of California, 2000 U.S. Dist. Lexis 13024.

34. "Memorandum for Selected United States Attorneys," October 19, 2009, http://www.justice.gov/opa/documents/medical-marijuana.pdf.

35. Office of National Drug Control Policy, "Fact Sheet, 2008 Adam II Report," 2008, http://www.whitehousedrugpolicy.gov/pdf/ADAMII_Fact_Sheet_2008.pdf.

36. Federal Bureau of Investigation, "FBI's Uniform Crime Report, Crime in the United States, 2009," 2009, http://www2.fbi.gov/ucr/cius2009/arrests/index.html.

37. Ethan Nadelmann, "Annual Report 2010: Making Your Voice Heard, Drug Policy Alliance," 2010, http://drugpolicy.org/docUploads/DPA_Annual_Report_2010.pdf.

38. Bureau of Justice Statistics, *Prison Inmates at Midyear 2009–Statistical Tables*, NCJ 230113 (Washington, DC: Bureau of Justice Statistics, June 2010).

39. Nicholas Casey and Jose de Cordoba, "Northern Mexico's State of Anarchy," *Wall Street Journal*, November 20, 2010.

40. Casey and de Cordoba, "Northern Mexico's State of Anarchy."

41. Guy Lawson, "The Making of a Narco State," *Rolling Stone*, March 19, 2009, 60.

42. James C. Howell and Scott H. Decker, *The Youth Gangs, Drugs, and Violence Connection* (Washington, DC: Office of Juvenile Justice and Delinquency Prevention, Department of Justice, January 1999).

43. Howell and Decker, *The Youth Gangs, Drugs, and Violence Connection*, 4.

44. Department of Justice, "Organized Gangs and Drug Trafficking; National Drug Intelligence Center, National Drug Threat Assessment 2006," January 2006, http://www.justice.gov/ndic/pubs11/18862/gangs.htm.

45 Jeffrey A. Miron, "Violence and the U.S. Prohibitions of Drugs and Alcohol," *American Law and Economics Review* 1–2 (1999): 78–114.

46. Jeanne Whalen, "In Quest for 'Legal High,' Chemists Outfox Law," *Wall Street Journal*, October 30, 2010.

47. Rebecca Cathcart, "Second Rail-Equipped Drug Tunnel Found at Mexican Border," *New York Times*, November 26, 2010.

48. United Nations, *World Drug Report 2011* (New York: United Nations Office on Drugs and Crime, 2011), 8.

49. United Nations, *World Drug Report 2011*, 15.

50. United Nations, "Illicit Drug Trends in Afghanistan," UN Office on Drugs and Crime, New York, June 2008, 8.

51. Jon Lee Anderson, "Letter from Afghanistan: The Taliban's Opium War," *The New Yorker*, July 9, 2007.

52. Rod Nordland, "U.S. Turns a Blind Eye to Opium in Afghan Town," *New York Times*, March 21, 2010.

53. United Nations, "Illicit Drug Trends in Afghanistan," 8.

54. United Nations, *World Drug Report 2011*, 65.

55. United Nations, *World Drug Report 2011*, 16.

56. Government Accountability Office, "Government Accountability Office Report: Drug Control: Interdiction Efforts in Central America Have Had Little Impact on the Flow of Drugs," Letter Report, GAO/NSIAD-94-233, August 2, 1984.

57. Public Broadcasting System, "Public Broadcasting System's Wide Angle Program," June 15, 2008, http://www.pbs.org/wnet/wideangle/episodes/an-honest-citizen/map-colombia-cocaine-and-cash/colombia/536/.

58. Evo Morales Ayma, "Let Me Chew My Coca Leaves," letter to the editor, *New York Times*, March 13, 2009.

59. United Nations, *World Drug Report 2011*, 175.

60. United Nations, *World Drug Report 2011*, 201.

61. Imogen Foulkes, "Ten Years on from Needle Park, February 4, 2002, http://www.swissinfo.ch/eng/Ten_years_on_from_Needle_Park.html?cid=2517882.

62. Robert Ali et al., "Report of the External Panel on the Evaluation of the Swiss Scientific Studies of Medically Prescribed Narcotics to Drug Addicts" (presented to the World Health Organization, 1999).

63. Urs Geiser, "Swiss to Agree Heroin Scheme but Say No to Dope," February 4, 2008, http://www.swissinfo.ch/eng/Home/Archive/Swiss_to_agree _heroin_scheme_but_say_no_to_dope.html?cid=7071120.

64. Public Broadcasting System, "Public Broadcasting System's Wide Angle Program."

65. See http://www.justice.gov/dea/demand/speakout/03so.htm.

CHAPTER 5

1. Thomas Kuhn, *The Structure of Scientific Revolutions*, 3rd ed. (Chicago: University of Chicago Press, 1996).

2. Jerome J. Langford, *Galileo, Science, and the Church*, 3rd ed. (Ann Arbor: University of Michigan Press, 1992).

3. Kuhn, *The Structure of Scientific Revolutions*, 52–56.

4. David L. Rosenhan, "On Being Sane in Insane Places," *Science* 179 (January 1973): 250–58.

5. Katharine R. Levit, *Projections of National Expenditures for Mental Health Services and Substance Abuse Treatment, 2004–2014*, Department of Health and Human Services Publication No. SMA 08-4326 (Washington, DC: Substance Abuse and Mental Health Services Administration, 2004).

6. Sheila B. Blume, "Treatment of Substance Misuse in the New Century," *Western Journal of Medicine* 172, no. 1 (January 2000): 4–5.

7. Nora D. Volkow, "Science v. Stigma," *Addiction Science and Clinical Practice* 4, no. 1 (2007): 2.

8. Institute of Medicine, *Dispelling the Myths about Addiction: Strategies to Increase Understanding and Strengthen Research* (Washington, DC: Institute of Medicine, 1997).

9. Center for Addiction and Mental Health, *The Stigma of Substance Use: A Review of the Literature* (Toronto: Center for Addiction and Mental Health, 1999).

10. Paul M. Roman and Harrison M. Trice, "The Sick Role, Labeling Theory, and the Deviant Drinker," *International Journal of Social Psychiatry* 14 (September 1968): 246.

11. Institute of Medicine, *Dispelling the Myths about Addiction*, 140.

12. Christina Hall, "Unholy Alliance: Big Tobacco and Big Government Join Forces," *National Review Online*. April 12, 2006, http://web1.nationalreview.com/articles/217312/unholy-alliance/christine-hall.

13. Elaine F. Parsons, *Manhood Lost: Fallen Drunkards and Redeeming Women in the Nineteenth-Century United States* (Baltimore, MD: Johns Hopkins University Press, 2003).

14. Sarah M. Tracy, *Alcoholism in America: From Reconstruction to Prohibition* (Baltimore, MD: Johns Hopkins University Press, 2007), 98.

15. William L. White, *Slaying the Dragon: The History of Addiction Treatment and Recovery in America* (Bloomington, IL: Chestnut Health Systems Publication, 1998), 9.

16. White, *Slaying the Dragon*, 9.

17. Robin Room, "The Cultural Framing of Addiction," *Janus Head* 6, no. 2: 229.

18. "Running to Rehab," ABC News, October 2, 2006, http://abcnews.go.com/Politics/story?id=2518173&page=1, retrieved February 3, 2010.

CHAPTER 6

1. Eric Kandel, James Schwartz, and Thomas Jessell, *Principles of Neural Science*, 4th ed. (New York: McGraw-Hill Medical, 2000).

2. Kandel was more honest a few years later in an interview with *Discover* magazine. He was asked, "What do you think researchers will find consciousness to be?" and he replied, "Oh, my gosh. I have no guesses. I think it's a very deep problem, and I don't really have any original ideas about that." http://discovermagazine.com/2006/apr/eric-kandel, April 2, 2006 (accessed February 11, 2010).

3. Nora D. Volkow, "Beyond the Brain: The Medical Consequences of Abuse and Addiction," *NIDA Notes* 18, no. 6 (February 2004): 3.

4. Alan I. Leshner, Testimony before the Senate Labor and Human Resources Committee, July 28, National Institute on Drug Abuse, National Institutes of Health.

5. Joanna S. Fowler, Nora D. Volkow, Cheryl A. Kassed, and Linda Chang, "Imaging the Addicted Human Brain," *Addiction Science and Clinical Practice* 4, no. 1 (April 2007): 4–16.

6. Eric J. Nestler and Robert C. Malenka, "The Addicted Brain," *Scientific American*, March 2004, 78–85.

7. Theodore Dalrymple, "Heroin Addiction Isn't an Illness . . . and We Should Stop Spending Millions "Treating" It." *London Daily Mail, Mail Online*, August 18, 2007, http://www.dailymail.co.uk/health/article-476208/Heroin-addiction-isnt-illness--stop-spending-millions-treating-it.html#ixzz1d2cm3T62.

8. Nestler and Malenka, "The Addicted Brain," 80.

9. Enoch Gordis, "10th Special Report to the U.S. Congress on Alcohol and Health," National Institute on Alcohol Abuse and Alcoholism, 2000.

10. L. Kaij, "Studies on the Etiology and Sequels of Abuse of Alcohol" (thesis, University of Lund, 1960).

11. H. Gurlling, R. M. Murray, and C. A. Clifford, "Investigations in the Genetics of Alcohol Dependence and into Its Effects on Brain Function," in *Twin Research 3, Part C: Epidemiological and Clinical Studies*, Proceedings of the Third International Congress on Twin Studies, Jerusalem, June 16–20, 1980.

12. D. W. Goodwin, F. Schulsinger, N. Moller, L. Hermansen, G. Winokur, and S. B. Guze, "Drinking Problems in Adopted and Nonadopted Sons of Alcoholics," *Archives of General Psychiatry* 31, no. 2 August 1974): 164–69.

13. Constance Holden, "A Cautionary Genetic Tale: The Sobering Story of D2," *Science* 264 (June 17, 1994): 1696–97.

14. M. K. Mulligan et al., "Toward Understanding the Genetics of Alcohol Drinking through Transcriptome Meta-Analysis," *Proceedings of the National Academy of Sciences* 103 (April 18, 2006): 6369.

15. William Sherman, "Test Targets Addiction Gene," *New York Daily News*, Health section, February 12, 2006. According to the article, Noble has a $35 saliva test that is sent to a lab for analysis. It is being developed by a West Coast pharmaceutical firm. Noble's research was funded by a $1 million grant from the Christopher D. Smithers Foundation.

16. Stanton Peele, "The Implications and Limitations of Genetic Models of Alcoholism and Other Addictions," *Journal of Studies on Alcohol* 47 (1986): 63–73.

17. L. A. R. Stein, John R. Graham, Yossef S. Ben-Porath, and John L. McNulty, "Using the MMPI-2 to Detect Substance Abuse in an Outpatient Mental Health Setting," *Psychological Assessment* 11, no. 1 (1999): 94–100.

18. I. C. Weaver N. Cervoni, F. A. Champagne, A. C. D'Alessio, S. Sharma, J. R. Seckl, S. Dymov, M. Szyf, and M. J. Meaney, "Epigenetic Programming by Maternal Behavior," *Nature Neuroscience* 7, no. 8 (August 2004): 847–54.

19. C. Rampon et al., "Effects of Environmental Enrichment on Gene Expression in the Brain," *Proceedings of the National Academy of Sciences* 97, no. 23 (November 7, 2000): 12881.

20. Abigail Zuger, "The Brain: Malleable, Capable, Vulnerable," *New York Times*, Books section, May 29, 2007 (review of Norman Doidge, *The Brain That Changes Itself: Stories of Personal Triumph from the Frontiers of Brain Science* [New York: Viking]).

21. For a review of these studies, see the *Time* magazine cover story of January 29, 2007: "How the Brain Rewires Itself," See also Jeffrey M. Schwartz and Sharon Begley, *The Mind and the Brain: Neuroplasticity and the Power of Mental Force* (New York: Regan Books, 2002), 217. See also Doidge, *The Brain That Changes Itself*.

22. E. A. Macquire et al., "Navigation-Related Structural Change in the Hippocampi of Taxi Drivers," *Proceedings of the National Academy of Sciences* 97, no. 8 (April 11, 2000): 4398–403.

23. Schwartz and Begley, *The Mind and the Brain*.

24. Suzhen Dong et al., "Environment Enrichment Rescues the Neurodegenerative Phenotypes in Presenilins-Deficient Mice," *European Journal of Neuroscience* 26, no. 1 (2007): 101–12.

25. Jeneen Interlandi, "What Addicts Need," *Newsweek*, March 3, 2008.

26. Patrick Kennedy, *Congressional Record*, March 5, 2008 (House), H1287.

27. Claudette Wallace, "Response: No More '28 days and You're Cured,'" *Addiction Science and Clinical Practice* 4, no. 1 (December 2007): 56. This was a roundtable discussion of the preceding article in the same issue by Michael Dennis and Christy K. Scott, "Managing Addiction as a Chronic Disease."

CHAPTER 7

1. American Cancer Society, *Cancer Facts and Figures 2003* (New York: American Cancer Society, 2003), 22.

2. Harry S. Warner, Rev. Francis W. McPeek, and E. M. Jellinek, "Yale Summer School Lecturers, Alcohol, Science, and Society, Twenty-Nine Lectures with Discussions as Given at the Yale Summer School of Alcohol Studies," *Journal of Studies on Alcohol* 1945: 381.

3. Lester C. Walker, "What We Know about Drinking," *Harper's Magazine*, July 1950.

4. George Vaillant, *The Natural History of Alcoholism* (Cambridge, MA: Harvard University Press, 1983). See also Stanton Peele's book review in the *New York Times*, June 26, 1983.

5. Herb Kleber, "Oral History Interview for the Univ. of Michigan," Substance Abuse Research Center, 2008, http://sitemaker.umich.edu/substance.abuse.history/home.

6. National Institute on Drug Abuse, *Drugs, Brains, and Behavior: The Science of Addiction* (Bethesda, MD: National Institute on Drug Abuse, 2010), 26.

7. One of thirteen principles in *Principles of Drug Addiction Treatment: A Research Based Guide*, 2nd ed., NIH Publication No. 09-4180 (Bethesda, MD: National Institute of Drug Abuse, 2009).

8. See preface to Alcoholics Anonymous, *Alcoholics Anonymous*, 4th ed. (New York: Alcoholics Anonymous, 2001).

9. Thomas Wiclkzer, Charles Maynard, Adam Atherly, Margaret Frederick, Thomas Koepsell, Antoinette Knrpsk, and Kenneth Stark, "Completion Rates of Clients Discharged from Drug and Alcohol Treatment Programs in Washington State," *American Journal of Public Health* 84, no. 2 (February 1994): 215–21.

10. D. L. Davies, "Normal Drinking in Recovered Alcohol Addicts," *Quarterly Journal of Studies on Alcohol* 23:94–104.

11. D. J. Armor, J. M. Polich, and H. B. Stambul, *Alcoholism and Treatment* (Santa Monica, CA: RAND Corporation, 1976).

12. In the HBO *Addiction* series, when asked about whether addicts have any personal responsibility for their behavior, NIDA director Dr. Nora Volkow claims that addicts must take responsibility for recognizing that they have a disease and for adhering to treatment.

13. Institute of Medicine, *Dispelling the Myths about Addiction: Strategies to Increase Understanding and Strengthen Research* (Washington, DC: Institute of Medicine, 1997).

14. National Institute on Alcohol Abuse and Alcoholism, *National Longitudinal Alcohol Epidemiologic Survey* (Bethesda, MD: National Institute on Alcohol Abuse and Alcoholism, 1992). Peele also discusses this at http://www.peele.net/lib/niaaa.html.

15. Lee N. Robins, Darlene H. Davis, and David N. Nurco, "How Permanent Was Vietnam Drug Addiction?," *American Journal of Public Health* 64 (December 1974): 38–43.

16. Alan Leshner, "Director's Column," *NIDA Notes* 11, no. 2, March/April (1996), http://archives.drugabuse.gov/NIDA_Notes/NNVol11N2/DirRep Vol11N2.html.

17. Karl Popper, *Popper Selections*, ed. David Miller (Princeton, NJ: Princeton University Press, 1985), 124.

18. Alan G. Marlatt, Barbara Demming, and John B. Reid, "An Experimental Analogue," *Journal of Abnormal Psychology* 81, no. 3 (June 1973): 233–41.

19. N. K. Mello and J. H. Mendelson, "Drinking Patterns during Work-Contingent and Noncontingent Alcohol Acquisition," *Psychosomatic Medicine* 34 (1972): 139–64.

20. Global Commission on Drug Policy, *War on Drugs* (Rio de Janeiro: Global Commission on Drug Policy, 2001), 13.

21. United Nations Office of Drugs and Crime, "World Drug Report 2010: Drug Use Is Shifting towards New Drugs and New Markets," June 23, 2010, http://www.unod.org/unodc/en/frontpage/2010/June/drug-use-is-shifting -towards-new-drugs-and-new-markets.html.

22. Talcott Parsons, "The Sick Role," in *Patients, Physicians and Illness*, 2nd ed., ed. E. G. Jaco (New York: Free Press, 1972), 101–27.

23. P. M. Roman and H. M. Trice, "The Sick Role, Labeling Theory, and the Deviant Drinker," *International Journal of Social Psychiatry* 14 (September 1968): 245–51.

24. Robert Rosenthal and Lenore Jacobson, *Pygmalion in the Classroom: Teacher Expectation and Pupils' Intellectual Development* (New York: Crown, 2003).

25. Ira J. Marion, "Methadone Treatment at Forty," *Science and Practice Perspectives* 3, no. 1 (December 2005): 29.

26. Center for Substance Abuse Treatment, *Overarching Principles to Address the Needs of Persons with Co-Occurring Disorders*, COCE Overview Paper 3, DHHS Publication No. (SMA) 07-4165 (Rockville, MD: Substance Abuse and Mental Health Services Administration, 2007).

27. American Psychological Association, press release, December 2, 2007.

CHAPTER 8

1. National Institute on Drug Abuse, "NIDA Announces Recommendations to Treat Drug Abusers, Save Money, and Reduce Crime," press release, July 24, 2006.

2. Government Accountability Office, "Drug Abuse: Research Shows Treatment Is Effective, but Benefits May Be Overstated," Report to Congressional Requesters, March 1998.

3. Government Accountability Office, "Drug Abuse," 17–18.

4. California Drug and Alcohol Treatment Assessment, "State of California, Evaluating Recovery Services: The California Drug and Alcohol Treatment Assessment, General Report," California Department of Alcohol and Drug Programs, 1994.

5. California Drug and Alcohol Treatment Assessment, "State of California, Evaluating Recovery Services," 71.

6. John B. Treaster, "Drug Therapy: Powerful Tool Reaching Few Inside Prisons," *New York Times*, July 3, 1995.

7. Institute for Research, Education and Training in Addictions, "Evidence Supporting the Public Funding of Addictions Treatment," http://www.ireta.org, May 13, 2003.

8. California Drug and Alcohol Treatment Assessment, "State of California, Evaluating Recovery Services," 21.

9. P. M. Flynn, S. G. Craddock, R. L. Hubbard, J. Anderson, and R. M. Etheridge, "Methodological Overview and Research Design for the Drug Abuse Treatment Outcome Study (DATOS)," *Psychology of Addictive Behaviors* 11, no. 4 (1997): 230–43.

10. R. L. Hubbard, S. G. Craddock, and J. Anderson, "Overview of 5-year followup outcomes in the drug abuse treatment outcome studies (DATOS)," *Journal of Substance Abuse Treatment* 25 (2003): 125–34.

11. P. M. Flynn, P. L. Kristiansen, J. V. Porto, and R. L. Hubbard, "Costs and benefits of treatment for cocaine addiction in DATOS," *Drug and Alcohol Dependence* 57 (1999): 167–74.

12. Constance Holden, "Is Alcoholism Treatment Effective?," *Science* 236 (April 3, 1987): 20–22.

13. National Institute on Alcohol Abuse and Alcoholism, press release, December 17, 1996.

14. Stanton Peele, "All Wet," *The Sciences*, March/April 1998, 17–21.

15. *Science News*, January 25, 1997.

16. R. B. Cutler and D. A. Fishbain, "Are Alcoholism Treatments Effective? The Project MATCH Data," *BMC Public Health* 5 (2005): 75.

17. Government Accountability Office, "Adult Drug Courts: Evidence Indicates Recidivism Reductions and Mixed Results for Other Outcomes," Report no. GAO-05-219, February 2005.

18. National Institute on Drug Abuse, *Principles of Drug Addiction Treatment: A Research Based Guide*, 2nd ed.. NIH Publication No. 09-4180 from the NIDA Notes (Bethesda, MD: National Institute of Drug Abuse, National Institutes of Health 2009).

19. Urban Institute, "Final Report, Findings from the Evaluation of the D.C. Superior Court Drug Intervention Program," http://www.urban.org/UploadedPDF/409041_findings.pdf, December 1998. See also Sally Satel and Frederick Goodwin, "Is Drug Addiction a Brain Disease?," Program on Medical Science and Society, Ethics and Public Policy Center, Washington, DC, 1998, http://www.sallysatelmd.com/html/20030420_DrugAddictionBrainDisease.pdf.

20. Sarah M. Tracy, *Alcoholism in America: From Reconstruction to Prohibition* (Baltimore: Johns Hopkins University Press, 2007), 119.

21. U.S. Department of Health and Human Services, *Projections of National Expenditures for Mental Health Services and Substance Abuse Treatment, 2004–2014* (Washington, DC: U.S. Department of Health and Human Services, Substance Abuse and Mental Health Services Administration, 2008).

22. V. C. Bunce and J. P. Wieske, *Health Insurance Mandates in the States 2008* (Alexandria, VA: Council for Affordable Health Insurance, 2008).

23. Government Accountability Office, "Social Security—Major Changes Needed for Disability Benefits for Addicts," GAO/HEHS-94-128, 1994.

24. National Survey on Drug Use and Health, *Results from the 2009 National Survey on Drug Use and Health: Volume I. Summary of National Findings* (Washington, DC: U.S. Department of Health and Human Services, Substance Abuse and Mental Health Services Administration Office of Applied Studies, September 2010).

25. National Institute on Alcohol Abuse and Alcoholism, *National Longitudinal Alcohol Epidemiologic Survey* (Bethesda, MD: National Institute on Alcohol Abuse and Alcoholism, 1992).

CHAPTER 9

1. William James, *The Principles of Psychology*, Great Books of the Western World, vol. 53 (Chicago: Encyclopaedia Britannica, 1952).

CHAPTER 10

1. Harry Quelch, "Socialism and Temperance Reform," *Social Democrat* 12, no. 1 (January 15, 1908): 1–8.

2. Jeffrey A. Miron, "The Tea Party and the Drug War," *National Review Online*, June 7, 2010, http://www.nationalreview.com/articles/229902/tea-party-and-drug-war/jeffrey-miron.

3. Alan G. Marlatt, Barbara Demming, and John B. Reid, "An Experimental Analogue," *Journal of Abnormal Psychology* 81, no. 3 (June 1973): 233–41.

4. M. L. Barnett, "Alcoholism in the Cantonese of New York City: An Anthropological Study," in *Etiology of Chronic Alcoholism*, ed. O. Diethelm (Springfield, IL: Charles C Thomas, 1955).

5. D. Cahalan and R. Room, *Problem Drinking among American Men* (New Brunswick, NJ: Rutgers Center of Alcohol Studies, 1974).

6. Stanton Peele, "A Moral Vision of Addiction: How People's Values Determine whether They Become and Remain Addicts," in *Visions of Addictions* (New York: Lexington Books, 1988).

7. Mike Gray, *Drug Crazy* (New York: Routledge, 1990).

8. David F. Musto, *The American Disease: Origins of Narcotic Control*, 3rd ed. (New York: Oxford University Press, 1999), 138.

9. William Jefferson Darby, Paul Ghalioungui, and Louis Grivetti, *Food: The Gift of Osiris*, vol. 2 (New York: Academic Press, 1977), 590.

CHAPTER 11

1. S. Satel, "Is Your Kid on Drugs? The FDA Makes It Hard to Know," *Wall Street Journal*, September 26, 1996.

2. See White House correspondence with the FDA at http://www.clintonlibrary.gov/_previous/KAGAN%20COUNSEL/Counsel%20-%20Box%20026%20-%20Folder%20002.pdf.

3. S. Levy, S. Van Hook, and J. Knight, "A Review of Internet-Based Home Drug-Testing Products for Parents," *Pediatrics* 113 (2004): 720–26.

4. See http://www.theantidrug.com.

5. M. Scarnier, T. Schmader, and B. Lickel, "Parental Shame and Guilt: Distinguishing Emotional Responses to a Child's Wrongdoings," *Personal Relationships* 16 (2009): 205–20.

CHAPTER 12

1. David B. Caruso, "Higher Cigarette Taxes Lure Buyers to Black Market," *Huffington Post*, April 10, 2010.

2. Mothers Against Drunk Driving, "Position Statement on Alcohol Assessment and Treatment," http://www.madd.org/about-us/position-statements/madds-positions-on-alcohol.html (accessed July 24, 2011).

CHAPTER 13

1. Mark Thornton, "Alcohol Prohibition Was a Failure," CATO Policy Analysis No. 157, July 17, 1991.

2. Richard Cowan, "How the Narcs Created Crack," *National Review*, December 5.

3. Ethan Nadelmann, "Let's End Drug Prohibition," *Wall Street Journal*, December 5, 2008, A21.

4. Monitoring the Future, *Monitoring the Future: National Results on Adolescent Drug Use: Overview of Key Findings* (Ann Arbor: Institute for Social Research, University of Michigan, February 2011).

5. Wesley H. Perkins and David W. Craig, "A Successful Social Norms Campaign to Reduce Alcohol Misuse among College Student-Athletes," *Journal of Studies on Alcohol* 67 (2006): 880–89.

6. Christie Barnes, *The Paranoid Parents Guide: Worry Less, Parent Better, and Raise a Resilient Child* (Deerfield Beach, FL: HCI Publishers, 2010).

7. David Segal, "When Capitalism Meets Cannabis," *New York Times*, June 27, 2010, BU1, New York edition.

8. Peter Temin, "The Origin of Compulsory Drug Prescriptions," *Journal of Law and Economics* 22, no. 1 (1979): 91–105.

9. *Time*, "Medicine: Massengill Pays," October 17, 2983.

10. H. M. Marks, 1995. "Revisiting 'The Origins of Compulsory Drug Prescriptions,'" *American Journal of Public Health* 85, no. 1 (January 1995): 109–15.

11. Temin, "The Origin of Compulsory Drug Prescriptions."

12. *Time*, "Medicine: The Thalidomide Disaster," August 10, 1962.

13. Read the story of "Krebiozen," a popular cancer treatment that had no therapeutic value but was wildly popular in the 1950s and early 1960s. View at http://www.quackwatch.org/01QuackeryRelatedTopics/Cancer/krebiozen.html.

14. Temin, "The Origin of Compulsory Drug Prescriptions," 9.

15. Marks, "Revisiting 'The Origins of Compulsory Drug Prescriptions,'" 111.

16. Kaiser Family Foundation, *Prescription Drug Trends* (Menlo Park, CA: Kaiser Family Foundation, 2010).

17. Ariel Nelson, "How Big Is the Marijuana Market?," CNBC Online, April 20, 2010, http://www.cnbc.com/id/36179677.

18. United Nations, *World Drug Report 2011* (Geneva: UN Office on Drugs and Crime, 2011).

19. P. M. Johnson and P. J. Kenny, "Dopamine D2 Receptors in Addiction-Like Reward Dysfunction and Compulsive Eating in Obese Rats," *Nature Neuroscience* 13 (2010): 635–41.

20. R. J. van Holst, W. van den Brink, D. J. Veltman, and A. E. Goudriaan, "Brain Imaging Studies in Pathological Gambling," *Current Psychiatry Reports* 12, no. 5 (October 2010): 418–25.

21. Y. Gao, A. Raine, P. H. Venables, M. E. Dawson, and S. A. Mednick, "Association of Poor Childhood Fear Conditioning and Adult Crime," *American Journal of Psychiatry* 167 (2010): 56–60.

22. Michelle Lodge, "Fearless 3-Year-Olds Might Be Tomorrow's Criminals," *U.S. News Health*, http://health.usnews.com/health-news/family-health/brain-and-behavior/articles/2009/11/17/fearless-3-year-olds-might-be-tomorrows-criminals (accessed June 20, 2011).

23. For an excellent documentation of this topic, see Robert Whitaker, *Anatomy of an Epidemic: Magic Bullets, Psychiatric Drugs, and the Astonishing Rise of Mental Illness in America* (New York: Crown, 2010).

24. Human Rights Watch, "U.S.: Number of Mentally Ill in Prisons Quadrupled; Prisons Ill Equipped to Cope," news release, September 5, 2006.

25. Doris J. James and Lauren E. Glaze, *Mental Health Problems of Prison and Jail Inmates*, NCJ 213600 (Washington, DC: Bureau of Justice Statistics, September 2006).

CHAPTER 14

1. United Nations, "Single Convention on Narcotic Drugs," http://www.unodc.org/pdf/convention_1961_en.pdf, 1.

2. United Nations, *World Drug Report 2011* (Geneva: UN Office on Drugs and Crime, 2011), 9.

APPENDIX B

1. Sally Satel and Frederick Goodwin, *Is Drug Addiction a Brain Disease?* (Washington, DC: Program on Medical Science and Society, Ethics and Public Policy Center, 1998).

2. Erik Eckholm and Olga Pierce, "Methadone Rises as a Painkiller with Big Risks," *New York Times*, August 16, 2008.

BIBLIOGRAPHY

Alcoholics Anonymous. *Alcoholics Anonymous.* 4th ed. New York: Alcoholics Anonymous, 2001.

Ali, Robert, et al. "Report of the External Panel on the Evaluation of the Swiss Scientific Studies of Medically Prescribed Narcotics to Drug Addicts." Presented to the World Health Organization, 1999.

American Cancer Society. *Cancer Facts and Figures 2003.* New York: American Cancer Society, 2003.

American Psychiatric Association. "American Psychiatric Association Position Statement on Substance Related Disorders," December 1995.

Anderson, Dwight, LL.B. 1942. *Quarterly Journal of Studies on Alcohol* 3 (December 1942). The *Quarterly Journal of Studies on Alcohol* is now published as the *Journal of Studies on Alcohol and Drugs* (http://www.jsad.com).

Anderson, Jon Lee. "Letter from Afghanistan, the Taliban's Opium War," *The New Yorker,* July 9, 2007.

Armor D. J., J. M. Polich, and H. B. Stambul. *Alcoholism and Treatment.* Santa Monica, CA: RAND Corporation, 1976.

Armstrong, Elizabeth M. *Conceiving Risk, Bearing Responsibility: Fetal Alcohol Syndrome and the Diagnosis of Moral Disorder.* Baltimore: Johns Hopkins University Press, 2003.

Ayma, Evo Morales. "Let Me Chew My Coca Leaves." Letter to the editor, *New York Times,* March 13, 2009.

Barnes, Christie. *The Paranoid Parents Guide: Worry Less, Parent Better, and Raise a Resilient Child.* Deerfield Beach, FL: HCI Publishers, 2010.

Barnett, M. L. "Alcoholism in the Cantonese of New York City: An Anthropological Study." In *Etiology of Chronic Alcoholism,* edited by O. Diethelm. Springfield, IL: Charles C Thomas, 1955.

Baumohl, Jim, and Robin Room. "Inebriety, Doctors, and the State: Alcoholism Treatment Institutions before 1940." In *Recent Developments in Alcoholism*, vol. 5, edited by Marc Galanter. New York: Plenum, 1987.

Beecher, Lyman. *Six Sermons on the Nature, Occasions, Signs, Evils and Remedy of Intemperance*. Boston: T. R. Marvin, 1827.

Behr, Edward. *Prohibition: Thirteen Years That Changed America*. New York: Arcade Publishing, 1996.

Blume, Sheila B. "Treatment of Substance Misuse in the New Century." *Western Journal of Medicine* 172, no. 1 (January 2000): 4–5.

Bonnie, Richard J., and Charles H. Whitebread. "The Forbidden Fruit and the Tree of Knowledge: An Inquiry into the Legal History of American Marijuana Prohibition." *Virginia Law Review* 56 (October 1970): 971.

Booth, Martin. *Opium: A History*. London: Macmillan, 1999.

Brown, Sally, and David R. Brown. *Mrs. Marty Mann: The First Lady of Alcoholics Anonymous*. Center City, MN: Hazelden, 2001.

Bunce, V. C., and J. P. Wieske. *Health Insurance Mandates in the States 2008*. Alexandria, VA: Council for Affordable Health Insurance, 2008.

Bureau of Justice Statistics. *Prison Inmates at Midyear 2009–Statistical Tables*. NCJ 230113. Washington, DC: Bureau of Justice Statistics, June 2010.

Cahalan D., and R. Room. *Problem Drinking among American Men*. New Brunswick, NJ: Rutgers Center of Alcohol Studies, 1974.

California Drug and Alcohol Treatment Assessment. *State of California, Evaluating Recovery Services: The California Drug and Alcohol Treatment Assessment, General Report*. Sacramento: California Department of Alcohol and Drug Programs, 1994.

Carpenter, William B. *On the Use and Abuse of Alcoholic Liquors in Health and Disease*. Boston: Temperance Society, 1861.

Caruso, David B. "Higher Cigarette Taxes Lure Buyers to Black Market." *Huffington Post*, April 10, 2010.

Casey, Nicholas, and Jose de Cordoba. "Northern Mexico's State of Anarchy." *Wall Street Journal*. November 20, 2010.

Cathcart, Rebecca. "Second Rail-Equipped Drug Tunnel Found at Mexican Border." *New York Times*, November 26, 2010.

Center for Addiction and Mental Health. *The Stigma of Substance Use: A Review of the Literature*. Toronto: Center for Addiction and Mental Health, 1999.

Center for Substance Abuse Treatment. *Overarching Principles to Address the Needs of Persons with Co-Occurring Disorders*. COCE Overview Paper 3. DHHS Publication No. (SMA) 07-4165. Rockville, MD: Substance Abuse and Mental Health Services Administration, 2007.

Clark, Norman H. *Deliver Us from Evil*. New York: Norton, 1976.

Cockburn, Alexander, and Jeffrey St. Clair. *Whiteout: The CIA, Drugs, and the Press*. London: Verso Books, 1998.

Conrad, Peter, and Joseph Schneider. *Deviance and Medicalization: From Badness to Sickness.* Philadelphia: Temple University Press, 1992.

Coomber, Ross. *The Control of Drugs and Drug Users: Reason or Reaction?.* Amsterdam: Harwood Academic Publishers, 1998.

Cowan, Richard. "How the Narcs Created Crack." *National Review,* December 5, 1986.

Cutler, R. B., and D. A. Fishbain. "Are Alcoholism Treatments Effective? The Project MATCH Data." *BMC Public Health* 5 (2005): 75.

Dalrymple, Theodore. "Heroin Addiction Isn't an Illness . . . and We Should Stop Spending Millions 'Treating' It." *London Daily Mail,* August 18, 2007.

Darby, William Jefferson, Paul Ghalioungui, and Louis Grivetti. *Food: The Gift of Osiris.* Vol. 2. New York: Academic Press, 1977.

Davies, D. L. "Normal Drinking in Recovered Alcohol Addicts." *Quarterly Journal of Studies on Alcohol* 23 (1962): 94–104.

Dong, Suzhen, et al. "Environment Enrichment Rescues the Neurodegenerative Phenotypes in Presenilins-Deficient Mice." *European Journal of Neuroscience* 26, no.1 (2007): 101–12.

Eckholm, Erik, and Olga Pierce. "Methadone Rises as a Painkiller with Big Risks." *New York Times,* August 16, 2008.

Edwards, Griffith. *Addictions: Personal Influences and Scientific Movements.* New Brunswick, NJ: Transaction, 1991.

Federal Bureau of Investigation. "FBI's Uniform Crime Report, Crime in the United States, 2009." 2009. http://www2.fbi.gov/ucr/cius2009/arrests/index.html.

Flynn, P. M., S. G. Craddock, R. L. Hubbard, J. Anderson, and R. M. Etheridge. "Methodological Overview and Research Design for the Drug Abuse Treatment Outcome Study (DATOS)." *Psychology of Addictive Behaviors* 11, no. 4 (1997): 230–43.

Flynn, P. M., P. L. Kristiansen, J. V. Porto, and R. L. Hubbard. "Costs and Benefits of Treatment for Cocaine Addiction in DATOS." *Drug and Alcohol Dependence* 57 (1999): 167–74.

Foulkes, Imogen. "Ten Years On from Needle Park." February 4, 2002. http://www.swissinfo.ch/eng/Ten_years_on_from_Needle_Park.html?cid=2517882.

Fowler, Joanna S., Nora D. Volkow, Cheryl A. Kassed, and Linda Chang. "Imaging the Addicted Human Brain." *Addiction Science and Clinical Practice* 4, no. 1 (April 2007): 4–16.

Gao, Y., A. Raine, P. H. Venables, M. E. Dawson, and S. A. Mednick. "Association of Poor Childhood Fear Conditioning and Adult Crime." *American Journal of Psychiatry* 167 (2010): 56–60.

Geiser, Urs. "Swiss to Agree Heroin Scheme but Say No to Dope." February 4, 2008. http://www.swissinfo.ch/eng/Home/Archive/Swiss_to_agree_heroin_scheme_but_say_no_to_dope.html?cid=7071120.

Gerber, Rudolph J. *Legalizing Marijuana: Drug Policy Reform and Prohibition Politics*. Westport, CT: Praeger, 2004.

Global Commission on Drug Policy. *War on Drugs: Report of the Global Commission on Drug Policy*. Rio de Janeiro: Global Commission on Drug Policy, June 2011.

Goodwin, D. W., F. Schulsinger, N. Moller, L. Hermansen, G. Winokur, and S. B. Guze. "Drinking Problems in Adopted and Nonadopted Sons of Alcoholics." *Archives of General Psychiatry* 31, no. 2 (August 1974): 164–69.

Gordis, Enoch. *10th Special Report to the U.S. Congress on Alcohol and Health*. Washington, DC: National Institute on Alcohol Abuse and Alcoholism, 2000.

Government Accountability Office. "Government Accountability Office Report: Drug Control: Interdiction Efforts in Central America Have Had Little Impact on the Flow of Drugs." Letter Report, GAO/NSIAD-94-233. Washington, DC: Government Accountability Office, August 2, 1984.

——. "Government Accountability Office Report: Social Security—Major Changes Needed for Disability Benefits for Addicts." Report GAO/HEHS-94-128. Washington, DC: Government Accountability Office, 1994.

——. "Government Accountability Office Report: Drug Abuse: Research Shows Treatment Is Effective, but Benefits May Be Overstated." Washington, DC: Government Accountability Office, March 1998.

——. "Government Accountability Office Report: Adult Drug Courts: Evidence Indicates Recidivism Reductions and Mixed Results for Other Outcomes." Report GAO-05-219. Washington, DC: Government Accountability Office, February 2005.

Gray, Mike. *Drug Crazy*. New York: Routledge, 1990.

Gurling, H., R. M. Murray, and C. A. Clifford. "Investigations in the Genetics of Alcohol Dependence and into Its Effects on Brain Function." In *Twin Research 3, Part C: Epidemiological and Clinical Studies*. Proceedings of the Third International Congress on Twin Studies, Jerusalem, June 16–20, 1980. New York: A. R. Liss.

Gusfield, Joseph R. Moral Passage: The Symbolic Process in Public Designations of Deviance." *Social Problems* 15, no. 2 (1967): 175.

Hall, Christina. "Unholy Alliance: Big Tobacco and Big Government Join Forces." *National Review*, April 12, 2006.

Hanson, David J. *Preventing Alcohol Abuse: Alcohol, Culture and Control*. Westport, CT: Praeger, 1995.

HBO. *Addiction. New Knowledge. New Treatments. New Hope*. 14-part series. Sponsored by the Robert Wood Johnson Foundation, NIDA, and NIAAA, 2007.

Hewitt, Brenda. *The History of NIAAA*. Washington, DC: National Institute on Alcohol Abuse and Alcoholism, 2006.

Holden, Constance. "Is Alcoholism Treatment Effective?" *Science* 236 (April 3, 1987): 20–22.

——. "A Cautionary Genetic Tale: The Sobering Story of D2." *Science* 264 (June 17, 1994): 1696–97.

Howell, James C., and Scott H. Decker. *The Youth Gangs, Drugs, and Violence Connection*. Washington, DC: Office of Juvenile Justice and Delinquency Prevention, Department of Justice, 1999.

Hubbard, R. L., S. G. Craddock, and J. Anderson. "Overview of 5-Year Follow-Up Outcomes in the Drug Abuse Treatment Outcome Studies (DATOS)." *Journal of Substance Abuse Treatment* 25 (2003): 125–34.

Human Rights Watch. "U.S.: Number of Mentally Ill in Prisons Quadrupled; Prisons Ill Equipped to Cope." News release,. September 5, 2006.

Institute of Medicine. *Dispelling the Myths about Addiction: Strategies to Increase Understanding and Strengthen Research*. Washington, DC: Institute of Medicine, 1997.

Institute for Research, Education and Training in Addictions. "Evidence Supporting the Public Funding of Addictions Treatment." May 13, 2003. http://www.ireta.org.

Interlandi, Jeneen. "What Addicts Need." *Newsweek*, March 3, 2008.

James, Doris J., and Lauren E. Glaze. *Mental Health Problems of Prison and Jail Inmates*. NCJ 213600. Washington, DC: Bureau of Justice Statistics, September 2006.

James, William. *The Principles of Psychology*. Great Books of the Western World, vol. 53. Chicago: Encyclopedia Britannica, 1952.

Jellinek, E. M. "Phases of Alcohol Addiction." *Quarterly Journal of Studies on Alcohol* 13 (1952): 673–84.

——. *The Disease Concept of Alcoholism*. New Haven, CT: College and University Press, 1960.

Johnson, P. M., and P. J. Kenny. "Dopamine D2 Receptors in Addiction-Like Reward Dysfunction and Compulsive Eating in Obese Rats." *Nature Neuroscience* 13 (2010): 635–41.

Jurkiewicz, C. L., and M. J. Painter. *Social and Economic Control of Alcohol: The 21st Amendment in the 21st Century*. Boca Raton, FL: CRC Press, 2008.

Kaij, L. "Studies on the Etiology and Sequels of Abuse of Alcohol." Thesis, University of Lund, 1960.

Kaiser Family Foundation. *Prescription Drug Trends*. Menlo Park, CA: Kaiser Family Foundation, 2010.

Kandel, Eric, James Schwartz, and Thomas Jessell. *Principles of Neural Science*. 4th ed. New York: McGraw-Hill Medical, 2000.

Keller, Mark. "The Origins of Modern Research and Responses Relevant to Problems of Alcohol: A Brief History of the First Center of Alcohol Studies."

In *Research Advances in Alcohol and Drug Problems*, vol. 10, edited by L. T. Kozlowski et al. New York: Plenum, 1990.

Kennedy, Patrick. Congressional Record: March 5, 2008 (House), H1287.

Kleber, Herb. "Oral History Interview for the Univ. of Michigan, Substance Abuse Research Center." 2008. http://sitemaker.umich.edu/substance .abuse.history/home.

Kuhl, Jackson. "Book Review: Eight Million Sots in the Naked City: How Prohibition Was Imposed on, and Rejected by, New York." *Reason*, November 1, 2007.

Kuhn, Thomas. *The Structure of Scientific Revolutions*. 3rd ed. Chicago: University of Chicago Press, 1996.

Langford, Jerome J. *Galileo, Science, and the Church*. 3rd ed. Ann Arbor: University of Michigan Press, 1992.

Lawson, Guy. "The Making of a Narco State." *Rolling Stone*, March 19, 2009.

Leshner, Alan. "Director's Column." *NIDA Notes* 11, no. 2 (March/April 1996). http://archives.drugabuse.gov/NIDA_Notes/NNVol11N2/DirRepVol11N2 .html.

———. *Testimony before the Senate Labor and Human Resources Committee, July 28, 1998*. Bethesda, MD: National Institute on Drug Abuse, National Institutes of Health, 1998.

Levine, Harry G. "The Discovery of Addiction: Changing Conceptions of Habitual Drunkenness in America." *Journal of Studies on Alcohol* 39, no. 1 (1978): 143–74.

Levit, Katharine R. *Projections of National Expenditures for Mental Health Services and Substance Abuse Treatment, 2004–2014*. DHHS Publication No. SMA 08-4326. Washington, DC: Substance Abuse and Mental Health Services Administration, 2004.

Levy, S., S. Van Hook, and J. Knight. "A Review of Internet-Based Home Drug-Testing Products for Parents." *Pediatrics* 2004: 113.

Lodge, Michelle. "Fearless 3-Year-Olds Might Be Tomorrow's Criminals." 2009. http://health.usnews.com/health-news/family-health/brain-and-behavior/ articles/2009/11/17/fearless-3-year-olds-might-be-tomorrows-criminals (accessed June 20, 2011).

MacLeod, R. "The Edge of Hope: Social Policy and Chronic Alcoholism in England, 1870–1900." *Journal of the History of Medicine* 22 (1967): 215–45.

Macquire, E. A., et al. "Navigation-Related Structural Change in the Hippocampi of Taxi Drivers." *Proceedings of the National Academy of Sciences* 97, no. 8 (April 11, 2000): 4398–403.

MADD. "Position Statement on Alcohol Assessment and Treatment." http:// www.madd.org/about-us/position-statements/madds-positions-on-alcohol .html (accessed June 24, 2011).

Marion, Ira J. "Methadone Treatment at Forty." In *Science & Practice Perspectives.* Bethesda, MD: National Institute on Drug Abuse, National Institutes of Health, 2005.

Marks, H. M. "Revisiting 'The Origins of Compulsory Drug Prescriptions.'" *American Journal of Public Health* 85, no. 1 (January 1995): 109–15.

Marlatt, Alan G., Barbara Demming, and John B. Reid. "An Experimental Analogue." *Journal of Abnormal Psychology* 81, no. 3 (June 1973): 233–41.

Marlatt, G. A. "From Hindsight to Foresight: A Commentary on Project MATCH." In *Changing Addictive Behavior: Bridging Clinical and Public Health Strategies*, edited by J. A. Tucker, D. M. Donovan, and G. A. Marlatt. New York: Guilford Press, 1999.

Mello, N. K., and J. H. Mendelson. "Drinking Patterns during Work–Contingent and Noncontingent Alcohol Acquisition." *Psychosomatic Medicine* 34 (1972): 139–64.

Miron, Jeffrey A. "Violence and the U.S. Prohibitions of Drugs and Alcohol." *American Law and Economics Review* 1–2 (1999): 78–114.

Miron, Jeffrey A. "The Tea Party and the Drug War." *National Review Online*, June 7, 2010. http://www.nationalreview.com/articles/229902/tea-party-and-drug-war/jeffrey-miron.

Monitoring the Future. *Monitoring the Future: National Results On Adolescent Drug Use: Overview of Key Findings.* Ann Arbor: Institute for Social Research, University of Michigan, 2011.

Mulligan, M. K., et al. "Toward Understanding the Genetics of Alcohol Drinking through Transcriptome Meta-Analysis." *Proceedings of the National Academy of Sciences* 103 (April 18, 2006): 6369.

Musto, David F. *The American Disease: Origins of Narcotic Control.* 3rd ed. New York: Oxford University Press, 1999.

Nadelmann, Ethan. "Let's End Drug Prohibition." *Wall Street Journal*, December 5, 2008, A21.

——. "Annual Report 2010: Making Your Voice Heard, Drug Policy Alliance." 2010. http://drugpolicy.org/docUploads/DPA_Annual_Report_2010.pdf.

National Commission. *The Report of the National Commission on Marijuana and Drug Abuse; Marijuana: A Signal of Misunderstanding, Commissioned by President Richard M. Nixon.* Washington, DC: National Commission, 1972.

National Institute on Alcohol Abuse and Alcoholism. 1992. *National Longitudinal Alcohol Epidemiologic Survey.* Bethesda, MD: National Institute on Alcohol Abuse and Alcoholism, 1992.

National Institute on Drug Abuse. *Principles of Drug Addiction Treatment: A Researched-Based Guide.* NIH Publication No. 99-4180. Bethesda, MD: National Institute on Drug Abuse, 1999.

——. "NIDA Announces Recommendations to Treat Drug Abusers, Save Money, and Reduce Crime." Press release, July 24, 2006.

——. *Principles of Drug Addiction Treatment: A Researched-Based Guide.* 2nd ed. NIH Publication No. 09-4180. Bethesda, MD: National Institute on Drug Abuse, 2009.

——. *Drugs, Brains, and Behavior: The Science of Addiction.* Bethesda, MD: National Institute on Drug Abuse, 2010.

National Survey on Drug Use and Health. *Results from the 2009 National Survey on Drug Use and Health: Volume I. Summary of National Findings.* Washington, DC: U.S. Department of Health and Human Services. Substance Abuse and Mental Health Services Administration Office of Applied Studies, 2010.

Nelson, Ariel. "How Big Is The Marijuana Market?" CNBC Online. April 20, 2010. http://www.cnbc.com/id/36179677.

Nestler, Eric J., and Robert C. Malenka. "The Addicted Brain." *Scientific American*, March 2004.

New York Times. "Scientists Launch Unbiased Study of Drink Problem; Form a Research Council to Amass Facts and Present Them for Discussion." *New York Times*, October 3, 1938, 1, 9.

Nordland, Rod. "U.S. Turns a Blind Eye to Opium in Afghan Town." *New York Times*, March 21, 2010.

Office of National Drug Control Policy. "Fact Sheet, 2008 ADAM II Report." 2008. http://www.whitehousedrugpolicy.gov/pdf/ADAMII_Fact_Sheet _2008.pdf.

Parker, James. "Inebriate Asylums, and a Visit to One." *Atlantic Monthly*, October 1868.

Parsons, Elaine F. *Manhood Lost: Fallen Drunkards and Redeeming Women in the Nineteenth-Century United States.* Baltimore: Johns Hopkins University Press, 2003.

Parsons, Talcott. "The Sick Role." In *Patients, Physicians and Illness*, 2nd ed., edited by E. G. Jaco. New York: Free Press, 1972.

Pear, Robert. "U.S. Seeks to Ease Process of Getting Disability Benefits." *New York Times*, April 8, 1994.

Peele, Stanton. Book review in the *New York Times*, June 26, 1983.

——. "The Implications and Limitations of Genetic Models of Alcoholism and Other Addictions." *Journal of Studies on Alcohol* 47 (1986): 63–73.

——. A Moral Vision of Addiction: How People's Values Determine whether They Become and Remain Addicts." In *Visions of Addictions*, edited by Stanton Peele. New York: Lexington Books, 1988.

——. "All Wet." *The Sciences*, March/April 1998, 17–21.

Perkins, Wesley H., and David W. Craig. "A Successful Social Norms Campaign to Reduce Alcohol Misuse among College Student-Athletes." *Journal of Studies on Alcohol* 67 (2006): 880–89.

Pike, Thomas P. *Memoirs of Thomas P. Pike.* Pasadena, CA: Grant Dahlstrom at the Castle Press, 1979.

Popper, Karl F. *Popper Selections*. Edited by David Miller. Princeton, NJ: Princeton University Press, 1985.

Public Broadcasting System. "Public Broadcasting System's Wide Angle Program." June 15, 2008. http://www.pbs.org/wnet/wideangle/episodes/an-honest-citizen/map-colombia-cocaine-and-cash/colombia/536.

Quelch, Harry. 1908. Socialism and Temperance Reform." *Social Democrat* 12, no. 1 (January 15, 1908): 1–8.

Rampon, C., et al. "Effects of Environmental Enrichment on Gene Expression in the Brain." *Proceedings of the National Academy of Sciences* 97, no. 23 (November 7, 2000): 12,881.

Robins, Lee N., Darlene H. Davis, and David N. Nurco. "How Permanent Was Vietnam Drug Addiction?" *American Journal of Public Health* 64 (December 1974): 38–43.

Rockefeller, John D. Letter to the editor. *New York Times*, June 7, 1932.

Roizen, Ron. "The American Discovery of Alcoholism, 1933–1939." Dissertation, University of California, Berkeley, 1991.

——. "Who Bought Whom? Revisiting 'Bowman's Compromise.'" June 10, 2011. http://pointsadhsblog.wordpress.com/2011/06/10/who-bought-whom-revisiting-%e2%80%9cbowman%e2%80%99s-compromise%e2%80%9d.

Roman, P. M., and H. M. Trice. "The Sick Role, Labeling Theory, and the Deviant Drinker." *International Journal of Social Psychiatry* 14 (September 1968): 245–51.

Room, Robin. "Sociological Aspects of the Disease Concept of Alcoholism." *Research Advances in Alcohol and Drug Problems* 7 (1983): 56.

——. "The Cultural Framing of Addiction." *Janus Head* 6, no. 2 (2003): 229.

Rosenhan, D. L. "On Being Sane in Insane Places." *Science* 179 (January 1973): 250–58.

Rosenthal, Robert, and Lenore Jacobson. *Pygmalion in the Classroom: Teacher Expectation and Pupils' Intellectual Development*. New York: Crown, 2003.

Rush, Benjamin. *An Inquiry into the Effects of Ardent Spirits upon the Human Body and Mind*. Philadelphia: Bartam, 1805.

——. *Medical Inquiries and Observations on the Diseases of the Mind*. Philadelphia: B & T Kite, 1812.

Samuelson, James. *The History of Drink: A Review, Social, Scientific, and Political*. London: Trubner & Co., 1878.

Satel, Sally. "Is Your Kid on Drugs? The FDA Makes It Hard to Know." *Wall Street Journal*, September 26, 1996.

Satel, Sally, and Frederick Goodwin. *Is Drug Addiction a Brain Disease?* Washington, DC: Program on Medical Science and Society, Ethics and Public Policy Center, 1998.

Scarnier, M., T. Schmader, and B. Lickel. "Parental Shame and Guilt: Distinguishing Emotional Responses to a Child's Wrongdoings." *Personal Relationships* 16 (2009): 205–20.

Schiff, Paul L., Jr. "Opium and Its Alkaloids." *American Journal of Pharmaceutical Education* 66, no. 2 (Summer 2002): 186.

Schwartz, J. M., and S. Begley. *The Mind and the Brain: Neuroplasticity and the Power of Mental Force.* New York: Regan Books, 2002.

Segal, David. "When Capitalism Meets Cannabis." *New York Times*, June 27, 2010, BU1, New York edition.

Sherman, William. "Test Targets Addiction Gene." *New York Daily News*, Health section, February 12, 2006.

Stein, L. A. R., John R. Graham, Yossef S. Ben-Porath, and John L. McNulty. "Using the MMPI-2 to Detect Substance Abuse in an Outpatient Mental Health Setting." *Psychological Assessment* 11, no. 1 (1999): 94–100.

Straus, Robert. "Problem Drinking in the Perspective of Social Change, 1940–1973." In *Alcohol and Alcohol Problems: New Thinking and New Directions*, edited by W. I. Filstead, J. I. Rossi, and M. Keller. Cambridge, MA: Ballinger, 1976.

Temin, Peter. "The Origin Of Compulsory Drug Prescriptions." *Journal of Law and Economics* 22, no. 1 (1979): 91–105.

Thomann, G. *Liquor Laws of the United States: Their Spirit and Effect.* 10th ed. New York: U.S. Brewers Association, 1893.

Thomsen Hall, Kathleen, and Paul Appelbaum. "The Origins of Commitment for Substance Abuse in the United States." *Journal of the American Academy of Psychiatry and the Law* 30 (2002): 33–45.

Thornton, Mark. "Alcohol Prohibition Was a Failure." CATO Policy Analysis No. 157. July 17, 1991.

Time. "Demon Exorcised." *Time.* March 14, 1938.

——. "Medicine: Massengill Pays." *Time*, October 17, 1938.

——. "Medicine: Keeley Cure." *Time*, September 24, 1939.

——. "Medicine: The Thalidomide Disaster." *Time*, August 10, 1962.

Tracy, Sarah M. *Alcoholism in America: From Reconstruction to Prohibition.* Baltimore: Johns Hopkins University Press, 2007.

Treaster, Joseph B. "Drug Therapy: Powerful Tool Reaching Few Inside Prisons." *New York Times*, July 3, 1995.

United Nations. "Single Convention on Narcotic Drugs." 1961. http://www.unodc.org/pdf/convention_1961_en.pdf.

——. *Illicit Drug Trends in Afghanistan.* Geneva: UN Office on Drugs and Crime. 2008.

——. *World Drug Report 2011.* Geneva: UN Office on Drugs and Crime, 2011.

Urban Institute. "Final Report: Findings from the Evaluation of the D.C. Superior Court Drug Intervention Program." December 1998. http://www.urban.org/UploadedPDF/409041_findings.pdf.

U.S. Department of Health and Human Services. *Projections of National Expenditures for Mental Health Services and Substance Abuse Treatment, 2004–2014*. Washington, DC: U.S. Department of Health and Human Services, Substance Abuse and Mental Health Services Administration, 2008.

U.S. Department of Justice. *Organized Gangs and Drug Trafficking; National Drug Intelligence Center, National Drug Threat Assessment 2006*. Washington, DC: U.S. Department of Justice, January 2006. http://www.justice.gov/ndic/pubs11/18862/gangs.htm.

Vaillant, George. *The Natural History of Alcoholism*. Cambridge, MA: Harvard University Press, 1983.

Valverde, Mariana. "Degeneration Theories." In *Alcohol and Temperance in Modern History: A Global Encyclopedia*, vol. 1, edited by Jack S. Blocker, David M. Fahey, and Ian R. Tyrrell. Santa Barbara, CA: ABC-CLIO, 2003.

van Holst, R. J., W. van den Brink, D. J. Veltman, and A. E. Goudriaan. "Brain Imaging Studies in Pathological Gambling." *Current Psychiatry Reports* 12, no. 5 (October 2010): 418–25.

Volkow, Nora D. "Beyond the Brain: The Medical Consequences of Abuse and Addiction." *NIDA Notes* 18, no. 6 (February 2004): 3.

——. "Science v. Stigma." *Addiction Science and Clinical Practice* 4, no. 1 (2007): 2.

Walker, C. Lester. "What We Know about Drinking." *Harper's Magazine*, July 1950.

Wallace, Claudette. "Response: No More '28 Days and You're Cured.'" *Addiction Science and Clinical Practice* 4, no. 1 (December 2007): 56.

Warner, Harry S., Rev. Francis W. McPeek, and E. M. Jellinek. "Yale Summer School Lecturers, Alcohol, Science, and Society, Twenty-Nine Lectures with Discussions as Given at the Yale Summer School of Alcohol Studies." *Journal of Studies on Alcohol* 1945: 282, 381, 463–64.

Weaver, I. C., N. Cervoni, F. A. Champagne, A.C. D'Alessio, S. Sharma, J. R. Seckl, S. Dymov, M. Szyf, and M. J. Meaney. "Epigenetic Programming by Maternal Behavior." *Nature Neuroscience* 7, no. 8 (August 2004): 847–54.

Weingarten, Gene. "Just What Was He Smoking." *Washington Post*. March 21, 1972.

Whalen, Jeanne. "In Quest for 'Legal High': Chemists Outfox Law." *Wall Street Journal*, October 30, 2010.

Whitaker, Robert. *Anatomy of an Epidemic: Magic Bullets, Psychiatric Drugs, and the Astonishing Rise of Mental Illness in America*. New York: Crown, 2010.

White, William L. *Slaying the Dragon: The History of Addiction Treatment and Recovery in America*. Bloomington, IL: Chestnut Health Systems, 1988.

Wiclkzer, Thomas, Charles Maynard, Adam Atherly, Margaret Frederick, Thomas Koepsell, Antoinette Knrpsk, and Kenneth Stark. "Completion Rates of Clients Discharged from Drug and Alcohol Treatment Programs in Washington State." *American Journal of Public Health* 84, no. 2 (February 1994): 215–21.

Woolf, S. J. "The Sick Person We Call an Alcoholic." *New York Times Magazine*, April 21, 1948.

World Health Organization. *Technical Report Series, No. 48. Expert Committee on Mental Health. Alcohol Subcommittee. Second Report.* Geneva: World Health Organization, 1952.

Zuger, Abigail. "The Brain: Malleable, Capable, Vulnerable." *New York Times*, May 29, 2007, Books section (review of *The Brain That Changes Itself: Stories of Personal Triumph from the Frontiers of Brain Science* by Norman Doidge [New York: Viking, 2007]).

INDEX

ABOUT THE AUTHOR

Michael J. Reznicek is a board-certified psychiatrist with over twenty years of experience. He has practiced in the military, in hospital-based community settings, in prisons, and in state hospitals. He currently practices as a psychiatric consultant in Washington state.

Dr. Reznicek has extensive experience in the field of substance abuse. He has written for *The Weekly Standard* and the *Omaha World Herald*. He has been a guest on numerous talk-radio shows at the local, national, and international levels where he has discussed drug abuse.

Dr. Reznicek is an outspoken critic of biological models of human behavior. He lives in Spokane, Washington.